FOREWARD:

Do you want your children to have a lot of options in life? Would you like for your children and grandchildren to be economically secure? Do you want for your children and grandchildren to struggle less financially in life than you have?

What if I told you that you could radically transform the course of your families finances over multiple generations without having a six figure income or a million dollar net worth? Building generational wealth isn't just for the super rich, in fact the benefits of building generational wealth are much higher for average Americans.

I truly believe it is possible for everyone in this country to get ahead and build wealth. We have more access to information and investing opportunities than any other generation in history. I grew up in a trailer park and watched as my parents were able to move up substantially over time in wealth. For most of my childhood they worked well north of 40 hours a week, with several years averaging over 60. My mom went to school at nights while working those hours to finish her Bachelors degree. They started with nothing (and had kids young), and retired early by our standards at 55, although my mom still works part time remotely. They were also able to cover a significant amount of college costs for both of their children.

When I moved out at 18 I worked at KFC for 3 years in Benton Harbor, MI. I met my future wife, Angie who had a young son. We moved into an apartment together for a year, then moved into her mom's basement for 6 months while saving up for a down payment on our first house.
We bought our first house shortly after I turned 20. It was a $48,500 foreclosure in Benton Harbor, MI. With 5 more years of working and saving we decided to move and found the perfect home a few miles away. Our house now is a 5 bedroom tri-level on 3 acres.

My wife and I have a total of 4 boys. Our kids are 18 and 13, and we have custody of our nephews who are 9 and 8. I'm in my mid 30s and work seasonally as a nuclear outage contractor. I work between 6 and 9 months a year, but during this time I am usually working 12 hour shifts 6 days a week. Although we were saving money in our early years together, we didn't start investing beyond Angie's 5% 401K contribution at work to get the employer match until 2013.

As our income increased we started saving more money in 2013 and I spent a lot of time learning about personal finances. I started writing about personal finance on my blog Action Econ in 2013 to share with others what I was learning. At the time I had a savings rate of around 20%.
Today our family is hitting a savings rate of over 40% on under $100,000 of yearly income. Action Econ is read by over 5,000 unique visitors a month from 111 countries. Thinking about money and writing these articles is perhaps one of the keys to our success. It keeps me focused on money and forces me to research new ideas and

to make greater effort to maximizing the utility of our money. Today I am much more focused on planning for my children's and grandchildren's finances than mine. This is a byproduct of building wealth; the more you build the further into the future you can look.

This book is about taking massive action towards improving your life and that of your children and grandchildren. If you are looking for a get rich quick scheme or a passive way to get ahead this isn't the book for you. Building wealth is done intentionally and requires massive action. You have to be willing to do more than the guy next door. You have to focus your thoughts, you have to put forth your creative energy, and you have to actually want it.

With 8% returns, starting at different ages, to get to $1 million at age 65 you would need the following:

How To Get To $1 Million At 65 Assuming 8% Returns

Starting At Age	Save Monthly	1 Lump Sum	Total of Monthly Savings
0	$38	$5,613	$29,640
5	$57	$8,362	$41,040
10	$85	$12,458	$56,100
15	$126	$18,561	$75,600
20	$190	$27,653	$102,600
25	$287	$41,200	$137,760
30	$436	$61,378	$183,120
35	$671	$91,450	$241,560
40	$1,052	$136,237	$315,600
45	$1,698	$203,000	$407,520
50	$2,890	$302,397	$520,200
55	$5,467	$450,524	$656,040

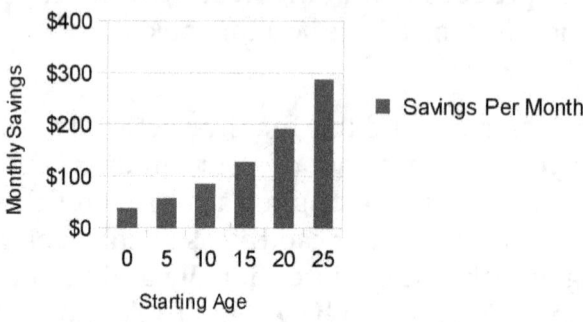

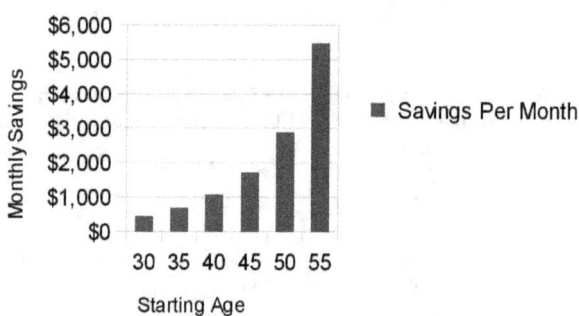

If I had realized when my children were born that just $5,600 could turn them into millionaires and effectively fund ther retirement I would have been much more focused on building capital early on.

ACKNOWLEDGMENTS

I'd like to give credit where it is due, this book wouldn't exist without the direct and indirect help of several people.

My wife Angie has been my wealth building partner from day one. She reigns me in when I get anxious and plan on doing something stupid, like investing all our money in gold, quitting my job too early, or buying a rental house that needs way too much work. She has had unbelievable patience with supporting my efforts to build my blog and write this book.

Mr. Verdonk for teaching me about compounding interest. This was my "aha!" moment almost 20 years ago that greatly influenced my long term wealth building goals.

Mr Sheehan for assisting me with becoming a better writer in high school. If I hadn't learned to produce written work quickly and with quality, my blog wouldn't exist, nor would this book.

My parents for their 3+ decades of hard work. I've had the privilege of living through upward mobility as my parents' careers improved and they built wealth during my entire childhood which saw us moving from a trailer park to a 1/3 of a million dollar home (which is a really nice home in southwest, MI.) Since my parents had us young my sister and I were able to see the entire journey. Parents who have children much later in life tend to already be established and their children grow up in a household that has already "made it". They challenged me to think of how I would earn $1 million vs. how I would spend it, because it's much, much easier to spend $1 million than it is to earn $1 million.

My sister Sarah for discussing finances with me even when I know it's not something she finds super interesting and of course for her help with editing this book.

Jon Wallace for making it possible for us to purchase our first home. In 2006 we had saved up 20% for a down payment, however Angie had some recent bad credit items in collections we had recently paid off and I had no credit history. Jon processed our loan application and at the time his business model was to originate the loans and package them for a big bank. Late in the process the big bank denied us. Jon said that we were doing all the right things and should be able to buy a house. He closed the loan and held the note through his company with the caveat that we had to refinance a year later. Without this help we would not have been able to buy our first house, which was a great home for us for 5 years and has become a rental property.

Ron Colvin for encouraging me to find some way to teach other people finances while we were discussing Obamacare details at the break table at work back in 2013. Without this urging I don't think I would have taken the leap to start Action Econ.

J$ from the blog Budgets Are Sexy, when I had been blogging in the dark for about 6 months and was close to throwing in the towel J Money shared one of my articles on Rockstar Finance. This one was on Floyd Mayweathers big payday and how I met Courtney Burton, a boxer from Benton Harbor whose early career mimicked Floyd's. When he shared that post on Rockstar Finance my blog traffic went through the roof, although the spike was short lived, several other bloggers started following my blog which also helped with keeping me going.

And of course, to my kids Drake, Trent, Arthur, and Jayden, the reason I am focused on building generational wealth, to open up as many possibilites as I can for them.

CHAPTER 1: THE PRINCIPLES OF THIS BOOK:

Someone is sitting in the shade today because someone planted a tree a long time ago. - Warren Buffett

There are several principles that I think are extremely important towards building generational wealth. All of these ideas need to be adhered to in order to build substantial wealth over the long term.

- Work = Money, Money can be spent, saved, or invested.
- The major differences between those who are wealthy and those who aren't are stock market participation, home ownership, marital status, and long term intentional planning.
- Every action you take should be to turn yourself from a laborer who sells his time for income into a capitalist who uses his money to earn his income.
- Wealth building is a team sport. It is highly important when in a relationship to be working in the same direction to the same sheet of music. It needs to be 100% buy in for all parties involved.

- Money is best invested over the long term and long term thinking is required.
- Financial Education is the cornerstone to any generational wealth building plan. Spend time every day increasing your knowledge on money management.
- We want to give our children the ability to do anything, but not so much they can do nothing. It does more harm than good to give an 18 year old $10 million.

Even with the best of intentions wealth acquired rarely lasts for 3 generations. Different sayings from around the world paraphrase this idea:

"Shirtsleeves to shirtsleeves in three generations."
"Rice paddies to rice paddies in three generations."
"The father buys, the son builds, the grandchild sells, and his son begs."
"Wealth never survives three generations."

The overarching goal of this book is not just to make life easier for your children, but to build a system where each generation is building up the next, with hard work, determination, and focus driving generational wealth building.

Understanding Compounding Interest:
Compounding Interest is the key to building generational wealth. Compounding interest is the interest your money makes on the money it makes. Compounding interest follows what's called the rule of 72. The Rule of 72 states that if you divided 72 by the interest rate you expect to receive, you will get the time it will take for your investment to double. If we expect a 7.2% return, then it will take 10 years for our investment to double. The Vanguard Total Stock Market Index Fund has returned an annual-

ized 7.23% over the past 10 years.

Rule of 72	
Rate of Return	Years To Double
3%	24.0
4%	18.0
5%	14.4
6%	12.0
7%	10.3
8%	9.0
9%	8.0
10%	7.2
11%	6.5
12%	6.0

Using the rule of 72 if you put $1,000 in the Total Stock Market Index Fund, in 10 doubling periods, or roughly 100 years, you will have over $1 million...but you don't have 100 years do you? You know what else, if you waited 60 years instead of 100 years instead of $1 million you would have just $64,000. What??? 60% of the time only gets you to 6.4% of the goal? What the heck?!?! That's the power of compounding interest, the heavy lifting is done on the backend.

To make this work in our favor we need to save extremely well early on. Saving to $64,000 quickly eliminated 6 of these 10 doubling periods on the way to $1 million.

Since we only have so many doubling periods available (generally 2 to 4) we need to focus on building up our nest egg extremely fast with savings. Here is a chart detailing these doubling periods, starting with $1,000.

Double Your Money	
Doubling Periods	Account Balance
0	$1,000
1	$2,000
2	$4,000
3	$8,000
4	$16,000
5	$32,000
6	$64,000
7	$128,000
8	$256,000
9	$512,000
10	$1,024,000
11	$2,048,000

What I'm telling you is that the goal of save X% is not going to work. Saving 5%, 10%, 20%, is not gonna do it when starting out. Yes, we always want to challenge ourselves to save a higher percentage of our income, but starting out we need to kick our savings into overdrive. Aim to knock out as many doubling periods as fast as you can in your investment account.

Here's the major opportunity for building generational wealth. If you can get some money, even a small amount invested for your children when they are extremely young, it will grow to a massive amount with a 50 to 60 year timeline, rather than the 20 to 30 year timeline we normally have for retirement savings.

> "The goal is not to be perfect by the end. The goal is to be better tomorrow." - Simon Senek

Investing more aggressively can also dramatically effect the doubling periods. If instead of averaging 7% returns in 1 total stock market index fund, you invest in small cap index funds, aggressive growth funds, and some individual stocks? Over the long term rather than a 7% return you may average closer to a 12% return. This cuts the doubling time down from 10 years to 6 years. Across a 60 year time span this means instead of having 6 doubling periods, you have 10 doubling periods. Rather than $1,000 turning into $64,000, it turns into $1 million!

Getting money invested for our children at as young of an age as possible, and invested in aggressive growth mutual funds and individual stocks will provide a solid foundation for building generational wealth.

To do this requires a shift in thinking. We need to apply a filter to all of our thoughts that is focused on the long term. We typically think in terms of the upcoming weeks and months, and not in terms of years and decades. The further into the future we can shift our thoughts, the more our actions will result in positive results in the future. We tend to over estimate what we can accomplish in the short term, but vastly under estimate what we can do in the long term.

CHAPTER 2: IS BUILDING GENERATIONAL WEALTH BAD FOR SOCIETY?

"There are instances of millionaires' sons unspoiled by wealth, who, being rich, still perform great services in the community. Such are the very salt of the Earth, as valuable as, unfortunately, they are rare." - Andrew Carnegie

The argument has been made that building generational wealth at its core is bad for society. It creates entitled people and ensures that all the wealth is hoarded by a few. This is far from the truth.

Wealth is Not Static:

Wealth can be created, the total wealth of the world is not a fixed pie. Wealth is originally created with labor and additive value. There is far more wealth in the world today then there was 100 years ago, or 500 years ago, or 1,000 years ago. The wealth of the world has been built up over time. This also has not been a steady increase. The world experienced a huge leap when the US was founded and a philosophy of self-government and freedom took root in the world. Free market economics creates wealth.

When wealth is created through capital investment more jobs are created and more people ultimately share in the wealth. Bill Gates made a personal fortune from Microsoft, but Microsoft's contribution to the world has far exceeded any personal wealth Bill Gates has gained.

Extrapolitive Wealth:

Wealth that is created can be extrapolative wealth that is based on increased valuations and not on increased cash generation. For example, Let's look at Apple stock.

Apple in July of 2020 was trading at $380 per share. In July of 2017 Apple was trading at $150 per share. This isn't a 253% increase in earnings. Although earnings did increase the valuation increased drastically. The price to earnings ratio increased from 16% to 30% during this time. This means that for the exact same asset, making the exact same amount of money, investors were willing to pay nearly twice as much for it in 2020 as they were in 2017. Increased valuations are a major part of the "Rich get richer" mindset.

Although the value of these assets has increased since other people are willing to pay more to own a piece of it, the true underlying value of the asset has not changed. The income from the asset has been static. Those with massive stakes in the business, like Warren Buffet who has nearly ⅓ of his Bershire Hathaway holdings in Apple may see their net worth skyrocketing, but if they sold any substantial amount of shares the price would plummet. It's funny money.

As of this writing, Amazon Stock is valued at around $3,200 or 92 times earnings. This is an extremely high valuation and is why Jeff Bezos is the wealthiest man in the world at $186 Billion. If Amazon were priced at a much more rational 10X earnings, Jeff Bezos would only be worth around $20 Billion. His income, or even his portion of net income that Amazon earns and retains, is far, far lower than many of the other people on the Forbes 400 list.

The super rich tend to have a lot of money invested in equities and when the prices of equities are driven up the price shows an increase in net worth, despite the underlying value, the income generated by the business remaining static.

Mismanagement Of Assets:

The premise that wealth always stays in families for several generations is wrong. The rich also don't alway get richer. We started this book with a series of proverbs about how the first generation becomes wealthy through the actions of a single person, the next generation lives off of that money, and the third generation must go back to working. For the vast majority of wealthy families wealth is not properly managed. Opulent spending, spending in excess of gains, and either poor investment choices or extremely cautious investment choices lead to dissolution of assets over time. Most 2nd and 3rd generation wealthy families expend more than they build.

Asset Dilution:

When people pass down great fortunes, those fortunes

get split along the way. A $10 Billion fortune split between 4 children becomes 4 $2.5 billion fortunes. That fortune split between 8 grandchildren becomes right around $1 billion each. Split among 16 great grandchildren is $500 million each, 32 great great grand children is $250 million each, and 64 great great great grandchildren is 32 million each. This assumes no one gave any money away, no one spent more than the growth of the money, and no one had bad investments. In the span of 5 generations The $10 billion fortune is diluted to less than $32 million per person. This takes only 100 years to happen.

There is "churn" on the Forbes 400 list. Take a look at the list today. How many Rockefellers, Carnegies, and Vanderbilt's do you see? These were the titans of industry in the 19th century and early 20th century and yet not a single one of their heirs appears on the Forbes 100 list.

A Net Good For Society:

For us non Forbes 400 people, building generational wealth is not about preserving or adding to a fortune of billions. It's not about ensuring our children and grandchildren never have to work and can live a life of luxury. It's about ensuring that they have the resources to do whatever their calling in life is. It's to ensure that any of the following are not seen as outlandish as living on Europa:

>   Owning a home
>   Going to college
>   Becoming a doctor
>   Having 4 children
>   Starting a business

It's about fully eliminating the scarcity mindset from your family tree. One of histories most important minds is Nikola Tesla. When Tesla stopped working for Thomas Edison after a disagreement over a bonus, Tesla worked digging ditches for $2 a day while trying to find support for his invention of an alternating current motor. The advent of the electrification of the world was put on hold for 2 years because a great mind had to dig ditches to feed himself.

"But inherited wealth reaches its utmost value when it falls to the individual endowed with mental powers of a high order, who is resolved to pursue a line of life not compatible with the making of money; for he is then doubly endowed by fat and can live for his genius; and he will pay his debt to mankind a hundred times, by achieving what no other could achieve, by producing some work which contributes to the general good, and redounds to the honor of humanity at large." - Arthur Schopenhauer

Bottom Line:

Generational wealth, even for the richest of the rich is not bad for society. Our children starting off with a few tens of thousands of dollars is also not bad for society. By opening up more options for our children and our grandchildren building generational wealth is a massive net positive action. Building generational wealth allows our children to make better decisions and to focus their efforts on purposeful work, rather than economic subsistence. With substantial assets they are more likely to become job creators than without.

CHAPTER 3: WHY BUILD GENERATIONAL WEALTH

Inherited Wealth may be something easily squandered, but inherited poverty is a legacy almost impossible to lose. -Eric L Haney

Breaking the cycle of poverty has never been more attainable than it is today. I love the concept of the rugged self made American, however I do find the way our society views wealth to be perplexing. We cheerlead for people to start businesses and make a better future for themselves, but once they are successful we vilify them as being the rich "1%". We then vilify anyone who receives any monetary advantage from their parents, and use this to take away from any success they build on their own. Do you know someone whose parents gave them a new car in high school? What did you think about them at the time? What about the kid whose parents paid for college? Or whose parents paid for his down payment on his house?

The truth is that life isn't fair, and that there will be no two children who have an equal amount of benefits or dare I say privileges as any other kid.

> *"A good man leaves an inheritance to his children's children"* - Proverbs 13:22

I think it's far more of a moral failing to send our kids out into the world with no eduction and no resources than it is to provide them with finance knowledge and financial assistance.

This book is focused on transformational assets, and specifically transformational assets at an early age. By focusing on investing in our children's and grandchildren' future's at a young age we not only leverage the power of compounding interest to our advantage we also completely change the trajectory of their lives. Transformational assets are assets that change the decisions and opportunities that are available to someone. Giving $1,000 to a 25 year old for a Christmas present is a generous gift, but if it is spent on a TV and Playstation 5 it is certainly not transformational.

An established nest egg is transformational. Down payment assistance to buy a first home is transformational, ensuring they end schooling without student debt is transformational.

These types of assets change the trajectory of a child's life. With no parental assistance in establishing assets early on, your child is likely to enter his or her 20s with significant student loan payments, as a renter, and with no nest egg. The problem is that instead of investing money in their 20s they will now be using the little income they have in their lowest income years to make student loan payments and pay more money as a tenant than as an owner. It may take a decade or more to be in a position to start saving and investing, all the while they are not building any equity and may be falling further into debt.

For a child who enters their 20s with no student loan debt, a nest egg of $10,000, a cash emergency fund, and enough down payment assistance to purchase a home the opportunities available will be vastly different. They will be able to start investing right away. Their home equity will build every month, they will be less likely to go into debt. They will also have a more stable foundation for their children. They will be able to have children earlier in life.

They will be able to take more career risks and seek better opportunities. These children will be able to build substantial wealth, far outstripping todays median and average wealth figures. They will also be able to help others a lot more because they will have extra income available and a higher net worth.

If a person starts investing in their 30s their money has about 30 years to grow before retirement, but if we adjust the system and have money invested for our children in their twenties, teens, or even in their single digits, the wealth will grow to exponentially higher amounts.

I focus a lot on the "how" of improving my finances and don't talk about the "why" enough. Let me tell you something, focusing on your **WHY** and thinking about your

WHY every day is what makes the HOW possible.

Ask yourself: "Why do I want to improve my finances and win with money?"

- *I don't want my heart to race when I open a bill.*
- *I don't want to feel like my world is falling apart because I don't have $400 for an unexpected expense.*
- *I want to have nicer things without guilt, whether that's a nicer car, new clothes, or turning up the heat 5 degrees.*
- *I want to be the first person in my family to be debt free.*
- *I want my children to have more opportunities than me.*
- *I want to ultimately retire with dignity.*
- *I want to retire early.*
- *I want to be a blessing and not a burden to my children and grandchildren.*
- *I want to give thousands of dollars a year to causes that are important to me.*
- *I want to change the course of my family tree.*
- *I want to ensure my children and grandchildren never live in poverty.*
- *I want to quit my soul sucking job and start my own business.*
- *I don't want to depend on anyone else, including the government.*
- *I want to inspire others to take control and win.*

Identify your WHY and reinforce it every day. Reinforce it when you take on extra hours or a side job. Reinforce it when you drive your hoopty for another year and when you cut your cable package. Tell yourself this is a small, temporary price to pay to fulfill your WHY. Knowing your WHY and believing in it is the key to winning with money.

Build Wealth As A Hedge Against Future Uncertainty:

In the history of mankind there have been 3 major disruptions in labor: The first was the agricultural revolution which turned hunter gatherers into farmers. The second was the industrial revolution which turned farmers into factory workers, and the third was the information age revolution which turned the factory workers into internet connected cubicle dwellers. The first transition happened 10,000 years ago, the second around 200 years ago and the 3rd 30 years ago. The fourth has slowly started and will take place during our children's lifetimes. The fourth is the artificial intelligence revolution. Note that these immense changes in the nature of work are happening at an increasing pace.

These revolutions ultimately created more jobs for mankind, and often in much better conditions, providing a long term better lifestyle. With each revolution there are many who were also left behind. These are the people who struggled to adapt to the changing landscape.

The amount of jobs currently done by people that may be replaced by AI in the not too distant future are hard to fathom. Some estimate that AI could replace up to 40% of todays jobs.

Our children need to be adaptable to change to a degree

that no group of humans in history has needed to be. They also need to start accruing capital and investing as soon as possible as a hedge against this future uncertainty. They are more likely than any generation in history to be without work for a long stretch of time and need to reinvest in their education to change career paths, perhaps multiple times during their lifetime.

CHAPTER 4: BUILDING WEALTH IN AMERICA

"It is clear that building assets does far more than simply adding money to bank accounts. Studies clearly indicate that families building assets experience more marital stability and move less, and their children perform better in school..." - Thomas M. Shapiro The Hidden Cost of Being African American

Where We Are At As A Country With Building Wealth:

Financially speaking, for the wealthiest country in the history of the world, we are not doing so great. I personally am appalled at the lack of financial education that occurs in our public schools. Our kids spend 180 days a year, 7 hours a day 13 years out of their lives at school and most schools never cover basic personal finance. The schools that do do so in a very limited amount. For me, when I was in high school we took 4 courses a semester in "block scheduling" with each class being 1.5 hours long for half the year. We had one class that was government / econ. For half of the semester, 45 days we covered econ, and for half of that time it was on micro economics. That's 22 days of 1.5 hours, or 33 hours out of 16,380 hours of primary education. This is not enough.

59% of households can't cover a $1,000 emergency. The average 45 year old only has $63,000 in retirement savings. This is not good. On top of that we spend 18 years taking care of our children only to launch them into the real world with no financial plan, no money, and we expect them to succeed? This is craziness.

Getting your money straight and taking some basic steps to helping your children get their money straight is not only an OK thing to do it is absolutely necessary. If you have a child who is struggling at 19, do you really want to see them still struggling at 29, or 39?

The true reason most people don't build any wealth is because they aren't actively trying to build wealth. Those who set goals and take action to build wealth tend to be successful, but the vast majority of our population is not actively trying to build wealth, we need to change that.

The Racial Wealth Gap:
I would be tone deaf if I didn't address this. As a white male writing a book about building generational wealth.

The median white household only has a total wealth of $111,146 while the median black household has a total wealth of only $7,113. That's a massive gap, but it also shows that neither group is doing well in building wealth. There are several causes to this that I can't do justice to in the scope of this book including our housing system, justice system, and our education system. The same study stated that it would take 223 years for this wealth gap to close.

72% of whites, almost 3/4 are home owners. Only 41% of blacks are home owners. This is huge when you consider that the bulk of household wealth in the United States is home equity. The home ownership gap is the biggest piece of the puzzle. According to the U.S. Census bureau the median net worth of someone at age 65 is $194,226, with $130,000 of that wealth being in home equity.

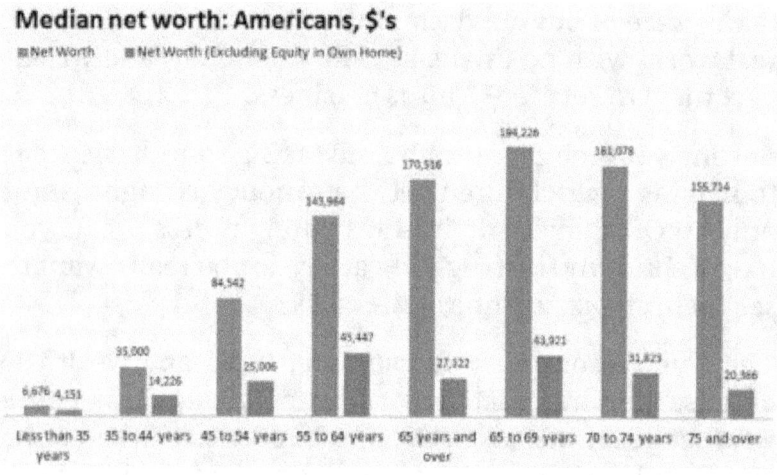

Which by the way, this illustrates a much bigger problem then the wealth gap between whites and blacks, Overall we as a rich country are ABYSSAL at building wealth. It's not like white people in America are doing all that great on building wealth either. You're looking at around $45,000 being the peak median non home equity wealth for households at any age in this country.

Not only does the wealth gap need to disappear, the targets we are shooting for need to be much, much higher. Black Americans shouldn't be aiming to build the wealth that white Americans have on average, and white Americans shouldn't be trying to get to the median wealth either. We should all be focused on blowing those numbers out of the water. To live off of $40,000 a year in retirement using a 5% withdrawal rate, we should be aiming to have $800,000 in non home equity wealth, this is over 17 times the peak median non home equity net worth.

According to a 2014 Federal Reserve study under 50% of workers had retirement accounts and only 13.8% of U.S. Households invest in the stock market directly (outside of retirement accounts). Black Americans with the same income as white Americans are 35% less likely to invest in the stock market.

This doesn't mean black people can not succeed. It means that there are legitimate structural problems and in our current economic environment black people need to be more focused and intentional than whites to build wealth. It also means that they should have a much larger motivation to change their family tree.

This book is not a policy book, this is for the individual. I have written in much more detail on the racial wealth gap and ways to fix it on my blog Actionecon.com. I 100% believe that if YOU decide to take action TODAY, YOU can change your family tree in under 10 years. This will not take 223 years, not 100 years, not 50 years, but 10 years. In fact you can change it tonight if you say right now that this cycle stops with me. That I will be the person who changes my family tree and I'm going to do it NOW.

CHAPTER 5: KILL THE SCARCITY MINDSET

"When resources are low or scarce, the rational decision is to take the immediate benefit and to discount future gain." -Mellisa Sturge Apple: The Color of Money.

The Scarcity Mindset:

As time goes on, constantly add to your emergency fund and strive to keep 3 months of expenses in cash. Building up a savings buffer of even a few hundred dollars to a thousand dollars can prevent the scarcity mindset.

Since long term planning is one of the largest keys to financial success, a scarcity mindset is one of the most dangerous barriers to this success.

"A state of scarcity is such a heavy mental burden that it can lead to temporarily lower cognitive ability and shortsighted decision making. This does not mean that the poor have less capacity, but that their capacity is overburdened because living

> *in scarcity takes up significant mental space and leaves less room for other mental processes. Those operating under the pressure of scarcity have been shown to eat poorly, parent poorly, make bad decisions, and even wash their hands less often. Scarcity also creates tunneling, which is a hyper focused mindset that homes in on the resource in scarcity."* –
> *Mehrsa Baradaran: The Color Of Money*

I need you to read that quote again. This is the mindset I want to ensure no one in my family tree ever feels again. It is such a waste of capacity to be stuck in a scarcity mindset.

As you build wealth your thoughts change, and your thoughts become action.

In 2009 in the middle of the great recession I was 23 years old, had a new baby, and was struggling financially. I counted on being able to work an extra 10 minutes each shift of the week. That would add up to a whole hour, which would give me the extra $7 I needed. I took a daily look at our electric meter and did everything I could to make it turn slower. I spent a ton of mental space on small problems. Let me rephrase, my problems that were large to me at the time, in the grand scheme of the world were small. I had significant time and brain power focused on stretching my $191 paycheck and reducing my expenses to under $191 a week.

Then as my income grew I was able to focus on bigger problems. Rather than thinking about the light bill I started thinking about different businesses I could start. I started thinking about saving for retirement. I started reading more. I started planning further ahead into the future. At first it was 3 months at a time, then shortly thereafter I was setting 6 month and 1 year goals. Now I set 10 year and 20 year goals. I read a ton more and can focus on long term ideas, rather than short term crisis.

It is unbelievably mentally draining to worry about these small personal economic issues. It's also a massive waste of brain power. I don't want to ever feel this way again, and I don't want you to either.

The decisions you make when under the scarcity mindset are always "penny wise and pound foolish." You're more likely to take on credit card debt, to finance small purchases, and to take greater health risks to increase your income.

At a minimum, building generational wealth is a tool to banish this economic trap from your life and from your children and grandchildren's lives.

CHAPTER 6: GET YOUR MONEY RIGHT

"Rich People plan for three generations. Poor people plan for Saturday night." - Gloria Steinem

The change starts with YOU. You have to focus on your money before you can make substantial progress on building generational wealth. You also have to take responsibility, and credit, for creating the change you want to see. Who the President is, who your boss is, what the unemployment rate is, what the stock market is doing, are all externalities that you don't have control over. Understand and accept that you are in control of your destiny and focus your energy on things you can control.

> *"Less financially able middle-class black families consistently give more financial asssistance to parents, relatives, and friends than their more capable white counterparts do." -Thomas M. Shapiro; The Hidden Cost of Being African American*

Having your money under control is the first step to

helping your children build wealth. Think about a young adult who is 25 who provides $300 a month in support to their extended family members. In just 1 year this amount of money would be enough for a 3.5% down payment on a $100,000 home. So in just one year, this parental support stopped them from transitioning from a renter to a home owner, which we already discussed is the primary source of wealth for most Americans.

Starting at 26 and going for 10 years, that $300 a month if invested at 8% average annual returns would grow to be $55,000 at 36 and if they never contributed another dime would be $555,000 at 65. A young adult helping her parents financially with a small amount of money could be the very thing keeping her from building wealth. This is why it is so important to first focus on your money in order to build generational wealth, to ensure you are not a financial drain to your children.

Long Term Planning:

This is perhaps the most important part of achieving any goals, and especially of achieving a goal as large as financial independence. You have to clearly define what you want, define the action steps to get there and measure it constantly. You have to be thinking long term. If you are always focused on this weekend you will never build for the next decade or the next generation. Most people think very short term. You have to think differently.

The best generational wealth you can give is to not be a burden to your children as you age. Take care of your money first before helping your children or grandchildren build wealth. There is still plenty that can be done to prepare your children and grandchildren to build wealth while still working towards building your own wealth.

Do Your Homework:

How often do you sit down and plan out what moves you are going to make with your money? What you are going to invest your money in and what you are going to invest your time and effort in and what the results will be? If you are like most people the answer is either never, or only once or twice a year. This should be done weekly, at a minimum. If you really want to change your family tree, if you really want to be the person in your family tree who destroys the shackles of poverty and mediocrity, than you must be willing to dedicate 2 hours per week of focused energy on planning for your money.

If the average person spends 0 to 2 hours a year planning for their money and you spend 2 hours a week, how much different do you think your results will be? Over the course of a year this is 104 hours vs. 2 hours. In the span of a decade it is 1,040 hours vs. 20 hours. Who do you think will be in a better spot?

This includes building a balance sheet and budget every month. This includes analyzing your income sources and figuring out ways to increase your income. This includes figuring out ways to decrease your expenses. This includes starting small businesses. This includes investing in real estate and managing your retirement accounts. This also includes planning for your children and grand children's financial future.

In addition to this period of planning you also need to read about personal finance. Allocate 1 hour per week to reading about personal finance. In a couple years you will be an expert. In Appendix I I have shared some books that I recommend reading.

Reduce Consumer Debt And Build An Emergency Fund:

Consumer debt like credit cards, store cards, payday loans, car loans, boat loans, and student loans take away from your ability to build wealth because it not only ties up your income in payments that often come with high interest rates, it also locks you into paying debt on assets that are decreasing in value.

When looking at your credit report, start with any negative charges on it, and call and offer to settle. Not only can you often settle for around 25 cents on the dollar, many of these debt collectors will also completely remove the account from your credit report. Although these bad bills can stay on your report for 7 years after paying for them, they don't have to. The owner of the debt can remove them. I recently had a gas bill go to collections after I missed the final bill before turning a rental property over to a tenant. I paid the amount in collections in full and they removed the negative account from my credit report in less than a month.

Save 20%+ For Retirement:

Saving 20%+ for retirement will ensure you have enough resources to retire and that you won't have to rely on your children or grandchildren for financial support. If you earn $50,000 a year and save 20% for 35 years, with no employer match and never getting a raise, earning 8% you would have $1.9 MILLION!

CHAPTER 7: MAXIMIZE YOUR SAVINGS RATE:

"The habit of savings itself is an education; it fosters every virtue; teaches self denial, cultivates the sense of order, trains to forethought, and so broadens the mind." -T.T. Munger

The next step is to think of ways to change the equation. The gap between income and expenses is all you have to build wealth. If the gap is negative or zero, then you will never build wealth. If the gap is $100 and you can find ways to increase it to $1,000 then you increased your family's generational wealth building by 10X! Become hyper focused on solving these math problems to increase the gap, your savings rate.

The difference between what you earn and what you spend, the delta, is what is left to save and build wealth. In America in 2013, the median household income was roughly $51,000, with an average savings rate of 3.9%, roughly $2,000, meaning the median American family spent $49,000. We will use these numbers to show the importance of increasing the delta to build wealth.

$2,000 per year invested at 8% per year for 30 years will result in $244,700. Not bad, but also not enough for a comfortable retirement. What if our average family earned 10% more and spent 10% less? Both of these are possible for most people. Working extra shifts, making some side money, or asking for a raise can all result in a 10% bump. Eating out less, packing work lunches, skipping Starbucks, cutting cable, shopping around for insurance, etc can result in these type of cuts, 10% isn't that much.

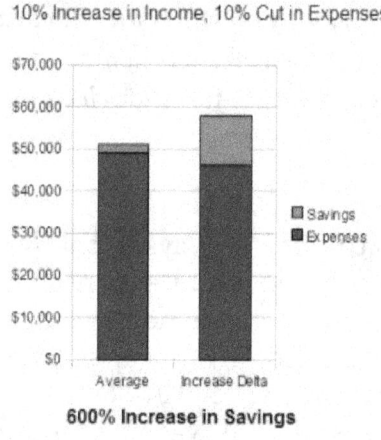

The new numbers would be $56,100 in income and $44,100 in expenses. Now this family has a delta of $12,000, a savings rate of 21.4%. **A 10% cut in expense and a 10% increase in income results in a 600% increase in savings, for the median family.** $12,000 invested a year for 30 years will result in $1,467,000. More important than the result of compounding the savings over time is that knowing you have this margin in life, allows for much less stress.

In our culture we tend to increase our lifestyle with every increase in pay, leaving us living paycheck to paycheck for our entire working careers. It doesn't have to be this way. Even if 10% isn't possible in your current situation, smaller changes make a big difference too. Even at 5%, income would be $53,550 and expense would be $46,550, Resulting in a $7,000 delta, a savings rate of 13%. Increasing the delta in your budget is the #1 way to build wealth. It really doesn't matter what you make, the only real metric is what you keep.

The average American budget after taxes spends 33% on housing, 17% on cars, 13% on food, and only 4% to savings. This shows that the main items to focus on for reducing expenses are housing, vehicles, and food.

Ways to increase income:
- Ask for a raise: By far the easiest way to increase your income is to ask for a raise. A 15 minute conversation can change your income drastically. On 3 separate occasions for 3 separate employers I negotiated a raise of $3/hr using the same formula: I asked my boss to have a conversation with me about my performance. I discussed my accomplishments and how I view my performance, and asked for feedback. I then asked what, if anything I could do to become more valuable to the company. Twice the employer offered me a raise right then. When I talk to an employer about a raise I approach it as a mutually beneficial meeting. Far too many people ask for a raise when they are angry, or flat out state they will quit if they don't get one, that

behavior paints you into a corner. A $3 an hour raise is $6,000 a year!
- Work more hours: Working more hours is always possible, we all have 168 hours a week. Remember this is only temporary. An extra 10 hours a week at $10 an hour is over $5,000 a year.
- Find a better paying job: How much time do you spend actively looking for a better job? If you are like most people the answer is under an hour a year. Spend 2 hours a week actively searching for a job that pays more. When you get the next job, keep up this practice. This falls in line with getting a raise being the quickest way to increase your income.
- Find a 2nd job: If you don't want to leave your current job, grab a 2nd job in the early morning, the evening, or the weekend. You could sort packages for UPS in the early morning, deliver Pizza in the evening or wait tables on the weekend.
- Create a side business/micro business. This self employed income can scale over time. Some examples are mowing lawns, babysitting, spray painting addresses on curbs, picking up trash in businesses parking lots, buying garage sale items and selling on ebay.
- Rent out a room in your house: You're already paying for your house, why not turn that liability into an asset? You can often rent out a room in a house for 2/3 or more of your total house payment. If your house payment is $1,000 a month and you can rent a room out for $600 a month you drastically improve your numbers.
- Become a 2 earner household.

Ways to decrease expenses:
- Move down in house. Housing is most Americans

highest expense often accounting for 33% of the budget. A bank will lend you 4 times your annual income for a house these days. If you stay in the 1-2X annual income range you will have a lot more peace and be able to build wealth a lot faster.
- Move down in car. Drive like no one else. Get rid of the monthly payment. I recommend having your car be worth no more than 10% of your annual income. If you are earning $50,000 a year, then its a $5,000 car. This is crazy to most people. What's crazy to me is paying a $700 a month car payment forever. As a note of practicing what I preach, I drive a 2001 Pontiac Montana. All 3 of the vehicles my wife and I own are worth less than 5% of our yearly income.
- Reduce taxes: Invest the savings you get in tax deferred accounts. If you get a 25% tax break for saving for retirement you get an extra 25 cents back for every dollar you save. If you save $10,000 that's $2,500 of real money you save on your taxes.
- Shop for groceries at Aldi and Save-a-lot. Use coupons. Meal plan.
- If you are a smoker, STOP. $8 a pack is roughly $250 a month, $3,000 a year. That's all money that could change your family tree. $3,000 a year for 40 years can absolutely change your financial life, your children's lives, and your grandchildren's lives.
- Increase insurance deductibles. Once you have a full emergency fund in place you can afford to take on more of the risk of a car accident or major home damage. Increasing your deductibles from $500 to $2,000 can save a ton of money.
- Pay insurance 6 months at a time, instead of monthly. Most insurance companies will give a decent discount for this.
- Switch to LED light bulbs. If you haven't done this,

it is a great way to save on your electric bill. LED lights are just as bright as incandescent or halogen bulbs and only use about 15% of the power.

CHAPTER 8: OWNERSHIP OF ASSETS

"Me owning all of my copyrights, me owning all of my shows, me owning every movie, me owning everything has put me in a position where not only can I have a studio where 9,000 people have come through the gates to go to work last year, but also to have generational wealth for my son and his children and if they manage it right after I'm dead and gone what that means is its passed on to so many people. So if you want real change, real change comes with ownership, so as long as you're renting the house and someone else owns it they have the power so that's what I'm trying to get a lot of us to understand." - Tyler Perry.

What is Wealth?

Wealth is any store of value that is accumulated overtime. Wealth can exist as static wealth or as income producing assets. Static wealth would be something like your home or a bar of gold. It has value if you sell it, but doesn't produce you any income. Income producing assets are things like stocks, bonds, rental properties, and royalty income.

The average millionaire has 7 streams of income. With building wealth the vast majority of your wealth should be in income producing assets and not in static assets. This way your wealth can compound. Whenever possible you want to protect these assets from taxation using tax favored investment vehicles such as 401k's and IRAs.

Build Wealth For Financial Freedom And Time:

Labor is the primary form of income that we all have, specifically labor for other people as employees. The primary goal of building generational wealth and setting our children up is to minimize the time they spend as employees and accelerate their transition from being employees to capitalists, who earn the majority of their income from their assets.

The idea that we should spend 2,000 hours a year working for others from 18 to 65 is not a historic norm, nor is it a desireable way for mankind to live. For most people to reach financial independence takes 20 to 30 years and they don't start the process until they are in their 30s or 40s, leaving very little time to enjoy the benefits that receiving income from their assets provides them. This is the fallacy of retirement.

If we can accelerate this process by starting saving and investing in their teens with high savings rates they could potentially reach full financial independence in their 30s and 40s, the same time their peers are only starting to build wealth. Fully taking advantage of compounding interest will greatly change the trajectory of your children's lives and your grandchildren's lives, and the amount of money needed to do this is relatively small.

The Spending Habits Of Those Who Build Assets And Those Who Don't:

How we choose to allocate our resources, both time and money, determine if we will ever become wealthy. On a balance sheet there are assets and liabilities with the net result being your net worth. On an income statement there is income and expenses with the net result being your savings rate.

Normal people will spend 60% of their income on needs, 35% on wants, and 5% will go towards saving and investing. As their income increases they will purchase more liabilities. A bigger personal residence, a new car, a motorcycle, a boat. These are all toys that come with a monthly payment and do not bring money into the balance sheet.

Somone who builds assets may spend 40% of his income on needs, 10% on wants, and 50% will go towards investing. He will constantly be working to increase his savings rate. As his investments bring in cash flow, those investments will replace his active income to cover his needs and wants, as well as continue to invest in more assets.

As a visual example of how normal people spend their

money look at this figure below. They earn their income from a W2 job and spend the vast majority of that income on liabilities, which come with monthly expenses.

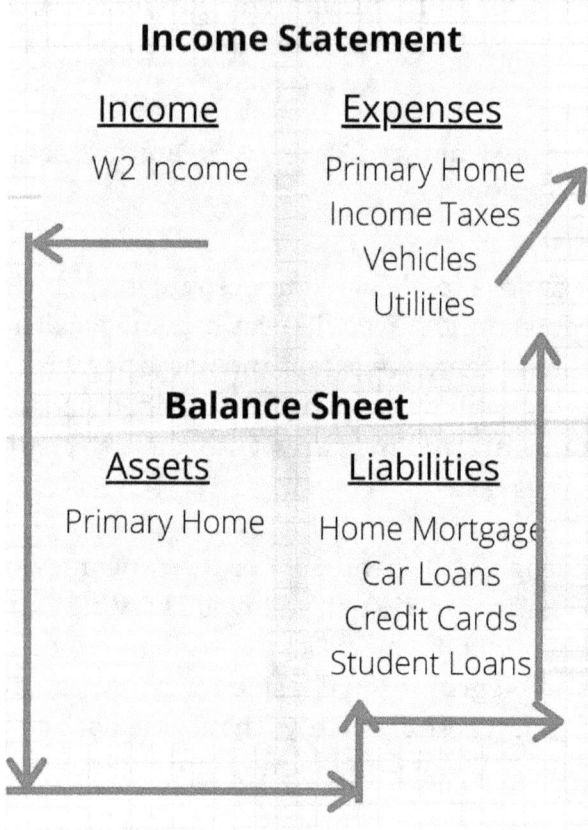

As a visual representation of the asset builder the vast majority of their income forms a symbiotic relationship. Their assets provide them with an income rather than a W2 job. They then use this income to buy more assets that generate more income.

Income Statement

Income	Expenses
Business Income	Primary Home
Rents	Income Taxes
Dividends	Vehicles
Royalties	Utilities

Balance Sheet

Assets	Liabilities
Primary Home	Home Mortgage
Rental Property	Rental Mortgages
Businesses	
Retirement Accounts	

CHAPTER 9: HOME OWNERSHIP

"We've seen such terrific growth in property values that it's hard for a person starting out to get a home - and I feel that home ownership is probably the single most important thing in keeping a family together. If you look at economic stability for a family, and being part of a community, home ownership is the number one thing that we should address." - Bruce Elder

Primary residence home equity is by far the largest wealth that most Americans have. The difference in rate of home ownership between white and black Americans also shows that home ownership is one of the primary causes of this wealth gap. The best time to go after home ownership is after you have paid off all your debt and established a 3 to 6 month emergency fund.

Buying a home is a major life step and is the cornerstone of the American Dream. Our society puts such a large emphasis on home ownership that we provide incentives to buy homes that in reality can set people up for the American dream to turn into an American Nightmare. Through the FHA people can buy houses with only 3.5% down, some people may even be able to get a 0% down payment. Incentives like these make people believe that they are ready to be homeowners when they are not. Often times these low down payment loans also may include higher private mortgage insurance, higher closing costs, and higher interest rates. Just because a bank is willing to loan you the money to buy a house doesn't mean that you should buy one yet.

As an example, here is a comparison chart of 4 different ways to obtain a loan for a $100,000 home.

	5% Down 30YR	20% Down 30YR	20% Down 15YR	20% Down 20YR
Home Price	$100,000	$100,000	$100,000	$100,000
Down Payment	$5,000	$20,000	$20,000	$20,000
Loan Amount	$95,000	$80,000	$80,000	$80,000
Term (in months)	360	360	180	240
Closing Costs	$3,000	$3,000	$3,000	$3,000
Interest rate	4.000%	4.000%	3.125%	3.750%
Monthly Principal and Interest	$454	$382	$557	$475
Private Mortgage Insurance	$102	$0	$0	$0
Total Monthly Payment	**$556**	**$382**	**$557**	**$475**
Amount owed in 5 years	$85,800	$72,200	$57,000	$65,000
Amount owed in 10 years	$74,600	$62,900	$30,400	$47,000
Amount owed in 15 years	$61,000	$51,400	$0	$25,500
Amount owed in 20 years	$44,500	$37,500	$0	$0
Amount owed in 25 years	$24,255	$20,400	$0	$0
Total Interest Paid	**$68,276**	**$57,500**	**$20,300**	**$33,800**

One of the most important details to me is what is the equity in the home 5 years out? The typical American family moves every 5-7 years, so knowing what you will still owe on that house in case you do need to move in this time frame is important. 30 year amortizations provide for a relatively small amount of money put on the principal during the first 5 years. This can be dangerous when paired with a small or non-existent down payment.

Principal Remaining On A $150,000 Loan

Years	30 Year	20 Year	15 Year
0	$150,000	$150,000	$150,000
2.5	$143,333	$136,793	$129,956
5	$135,943	$122,291	$108,151
7.5	$127,752	$106,366	$84,428
10	$118,672	$88,878	$58,621
12.5	$108,609	$69,675	$30,544
15	$97,453	$48,587	$0
17.5	$85,089	$25,429	
20	$71,383	$0	
22.5	$56,192		
25	$39,353		
27.5	$20,688		
30	$0		

When selling a home, the seller typically has closing costs of 3-5%, plus Realtor fees of 7%, at a minimum. In order to cover roughly 11% of the value of the home, there has to be significant equity or you could be stuck. Paying a large down payment and getting a shorter term ensure that you will not be upside down when you need to sell the home.

In the above chart, putting 5% down and getting a 30 year mortgage results in still owing $85,000 on the home in 5 years. After paying 11% in closing costs, this only leaves about $4,000, assuming the house sells for $100,000, but that is no guarantee. What's really interesting is due to a lower loan amount, a reduced interest rate, and no PMI, the payment on a 15 year with a 20% down payment results in the same monthly mortgage payment. 5 years into the 15 year mortgage only $57,000 is owed, even if the market dropped 30% you could still sell the home and walk away with cash in your pocket!

The monthly payments on a 20 year mortgage are substantially less than a 15 year and it builds equity much faster than a 30 year. A 20 year mortgage is a far better option than a 30 year.

The chart above demonstrates why putting down 20% and getting a shorter mortgage term are highly beneficial, build wealth quicker, AND greatly reduce your financial risk. It is also important to look at several lenders to see where you can get the best deal, since closing costs and interest rates vary widely.

The Checklist For First Time Home Buyers:

Lifestyle Prepared:

- Plan on staying in the home for at least 5 years.
- Know some basic home maintenance skills.
- Have stable, long term employment.
- Have a stable relationship with anyone who is buying the home with you.

Financially Prepared:

- Steady income for 3 years.
- No debts in collections.
- No current debt payments (car payments, credit card payments, etc.).
- 6 months of base expenses cash emergency fund.
- 20% Down payment.
- Can get pre-approved by a lender.

General Guidelines For Monetary Ratios:

- 15 year or 20 year mortgage with a payment less than 1 weeks take home pay.

- Ability to afford the home based on a 35% after tax metric on your own if your spouse/partner were to leave.

Additional Home Buying Tips:

Do not underestimate the value of a home inspection and septic inspection. These are relatively inexpensive and worth every penny. Never put in an offer without checking the boxes for requiring every inspection available. (Home inspection, Septic Inspection, Well inspection, etc.)

30 yr mortgage vs. 15 year mortgage:
A 15 year has a slightly lower interest rate. The higher monthly payments also force you to buy less house and to save money in your home equity. Most people who advocate for going with a 30 year mortgage and investing the difference don't actually invest the difference. A 15 year mortgage is also important for a diversification of investments. Paying down on your house may only get you a 3.5% return, but it is a guaranteed return and helps balance the risk of your retirement investments.

Keeping your house payment below 25% of your take home pay is another important metric to follow. Being at 25% (including taxes and insurance) ensures that you are saving 7% of your income compared to the average family. Shooting to be at 20% is an even better target. The less you spend on your house the more money you have for investing, and the quicker you can get it paid off.

Barriers to Home Ownership:

The two primary barriers that keep people from buying a

home are credit score and down payment. Before buying a home you should have a 3-6 month emergency fund built up and have paid off all consumer debt.

Credit Score:
- Keep your bills current
- Look up your Annual Credit Report and pay off back debt
- Reduce credit utilization
- Don't apply for any new credit within a year of applying for mortgage

Down Payment:
Although I recommend saving up a 20% down payment, it is still significantly better to do a smaller down payment as long as you get a 15 year mortgage than to get a 30 year mortgage with a 20% down payment. **Get a 15 year mortgage!**

Buy A Duplex:
Conforming loans, loans that most banks are willing to issue including FHA loans, are for principal residences only, however a duplex and even a fourplex will count as a principal residence so long as the buyer is going to live in the property.

This is a great way to build wealth right off the bat. Consider buying a Duplex that the total cost is still only 25% of your take home pay on a 15 year mortgage. There are many markets where this is possible.

In Indianapolis, IN you can get a move in ready duplex for around $60,000 or a really nice one for $90,000.

Now the numbers:
A $60,000 house with 3.5% down at 3% interest is $400 per month in principal and interest payments on a 15

year loan. Add in $150 for insurance, taxes, and PMI to get a total payment of $550. Total after tax income needed is $2,200 per month. If your household is bringing in around $30,000 a year in gross income you can afford to do this!

The beauty comes in with renting the other side out. You can rent out the other side for $650 a month and live for free! Your tenant is paying the entire mortgage and in 15 years the house is paid off even if you never pay any extra on it. This frees up 25% of your income to invest and build wealth right away!

What about a fourplex?
Fourplex's are harder to find, however they can also be an excellent deal, provided that you can afford it on under 33% of your take home pay. For a fourplex I'm okay with going up to 33% because the potential rental income is higher. This is the upper level for a single family home, so this is to provide margin if no rents come in. If no rents come in at all, you should still be able to afford your home.

The best deal I could find on a fourplex in Indianapolis, IN was for $140,000. This is still far less than what most people spend on a primary residence. A $140,000 house with a 3.5% down payment on a 15 year mortgage at 3% would require $4,900 down and would have a monthly principal and interest payment of $933 per month. Add in $200 for PMI, taxes, and interest and you have $1,133 per month. Total yearly gross income should be around $45,000 to afford this house.

Now, renting out 3 units at $650 per month should provide $1,950 in rental income, covering your entire house payment and giving you an additional $817 per month to invest!

CHAPTER 10: STOCK OWNERSHIP:

"The stock market is a device for transferring money from the impatient to the patient." - Warren Buffett

What Are Stocks?

Stocks are ownership in publicly traded companies. Stock ownership is how the vast majority of millionaires in this country built their wealth. When a company needs to raise money to grow it will sell shares in the ownership of the company in what is called an IPO or an Initial Public Offering. After this offering the people who own shares of the company can buy and sell them on the open market. Generally speaking, as a company grows and becomes more profitable the share price increases. If the company has more profits than they can reasonably re-invest in the business they issue dividends to share holders, a distribution of profits.

Diversification

Owning stock in only 1 or 2 companies is extremely risky. This is why mutual funds were created. Mutual funds buy small pieces of several different stocks. Some mutual funds are professionally managed and come with high fees, while others are considered index funds and have much lower fees. An index fund essentially buys a representation of all of the stocks on the stock market. Index funds outperform managed funds 71% of the time.

I invest primarily in index funds. The exact funds you choose are not as important as the amount of money you invest. If you are willing to research individual stocks, investing some of your money into individual growth stocks is not a bad idea, provided you fully understand the companies and the risks involved. Currently I split my investments with 75% going into mutual funds and 25% into individual stocks.

Here's The Index Funds I Invest In:

- **Vanguard Total Stock Market Index Fund:** Exposure to a weighted average of US stocks, heavy in Large cap companies. Large Cap companies are those valued over $10 Billion. (13.48% annualized return over 10 years)
- **Vanguard Mid Cap Index Fund:** Invests in middle sized companies valued between $2 Billion and $10 Billion. (11.97% annualized return over 10 years)
- **Vanguard Small Cap Index Fund:** Invests in small companies with values < $2 Billion. (10.95% annualized return over 10 years)
- **Vanguard Total International Index Fund:** Invests

in stocks all over the world, excluding the US. (4.28% annualized return over 10 years)
- **Vanguard International Growth Index Fund:** Invests in non US stocks with rapid growth. (10.79% annualized return over 10 years)
- **Vanguard Emerging Markets Index Fund:** Invests in Emerging Markets, such as Brazil, Russia, Taiwan, India, and China. (2.26% annualized return over 10 years)

Tax Advantages And Incentives:

The most common method to invest in stocks is through an employer sponsored 401K plan or an Individual Retirement Accont (IRA). Look at these as different folders that the stocks are held in, and these folders each have a different set of rules, some are beneficial and some are detrimental.

Traditional Vs. Roth:

Traditional accounts are the default that most people choose. With these accounts you get a tax deduction on the contribution now, the money grows in the account tax free, and then when you withdrawal it in retirement you pay ordinary income taxes on it.

Traditional accounts require a minimum annual distribution based on age started at 72.

With a Roth account you do not get a tax break now, the money still grows tax free and when you withdrawal it in retirement there are no income taxes owed.

Roth accounts do not have required minimum distributions. I personally like Roth accounts because future tax rates are unknown, so a traditional IRA's and 401K's true value can decrease if tax rates increase in the future. With a Roth account we know the future tax rate is zero. I would much rather pay tax on a much smaller amount of money now when I know the tax rate, than on a much bigger pile of money 40 years in the future with unknown tax rates.

Account Types:

401K Accounts: 401K accounts can be either traditional or Roth. Most employers offer both. 401K accounts come with the unique advantage of being linked to your paycheck. You set how much you want to contribute as a percentage of your pay and it will automatically come out of your paycheck.

The downside to 401Ks is that they often have a small variety of investment options. Most plans have somewhere between 6 and 20 mutual funds that you can choose from. Some plans offer an option called a self directed 401K where you can invest in virtually any stock or mutual fund that exists.

Currently 401Ks have a maximum yearly contribution of $19,500.

IRAs: Individual retirement accounts are accounts that you set up with a brokerage firm and contribue to on your own. You can make contributions whenever you want through out the year and can also set yup automatic contributions from your bank account. With an IRA you have much wider investment options than with a 401K plan. You can set up a traditional or Roth IRA.

Currently the maximum yearly contribution for IRAs is $6,000. There are limits on this for higher earners.

Health Savings Accounts: Health Savings Accounts are investment accounts that can be set up by anyone with a qualifying high deductible healthcare plan. They function similarly to an IRA in that you get a tax deduction for contributions and the money grows tax free. At 65 withdraws can be taken and you only pay your ordinary income tax rate on them.

The Health Savings Account however has one function similar to the Roth IRA: For qualified medical expenses, you can take tax free withdrawals at any time. This double tax advantage makes Health Savings Accounts a great way to build wealth.

Health savings accounts are sometimes sponsored through your employer, and when they are they get an additional tax benefit where contributions are exempt from Social Security taxes. For an individual plan that is not sponsored through your employer there is no Social Security deduction.

Health Savings accounts are similar to 401Ks in that they

often have a small selection of mutual funds to choose from. I personally use healthsavings.com because they offer most Vanguard index funds.

Taxable Brokerage Accounts: A taxable brokerage account is just what it sounds like, An account with no special tax treatment. This may sound like a bad deal, however a taxable brokerage account can make sense for many people.

There is no tax deduction for investments made to a taxable brokerage account. Inside of a taxable brokerage account any transactions you make will trigger a capital gain or a capital loss. These transactions will lead to the potential for a yearly tax consequence, even if you re-invest in something else.

These gains and losses are separated into short term and long term. gains and losses can offset each other, for example if you have a long term gain of $5,000 from selling one asset, but also have a $5,000 loss from selling another asset they would cancel out.

short term capital gains are taxed as ordinary income at your normal rates. short term capital gains are any gains on investments held for under 1 year. Long term capital gains are for any assets held for over 1 year. Long term capital gains have a separate tax bracket at a much lower rate than earned income. For taxpayers in the 12% bracket or less the long term capital gains tax is 0%. It increases to a current maximum of 20% based on income level, which is much less than ordinary income tax rates.

There are also advanced strategies such as tax gain harvesting and tax loss harvesting that allow investors to minimize thier tax bills over time.

UGMA Accounts: Universal Gift To Minor Accounts are taxable brokerage accounts that are in the name of a minor. They work exactly as taxable brokerage accounts work. These can be set up for any minor children.

529 Plans: 529 Plans exist as a savings vehicle for college expenses. Most of the time when people are referring to a college fund they are talking about a 529 plan. 529 plans are just like UGMAs, except they have a few small tax benefits and some extra restrictions on them.

CHAPTER 11: ESTATE PLANNING

"Only put off until tomorrow what you are willing to die having left undone." - Pablo Picasso

Beneficiary Lines:
Always fill out primary and secondary beneficiary information for all of your accounts. If you have major life events such as you remarry or have more children update these beneficiary lines. You would not believe how many ex wives end up with retirement accounts because their ex husbands never thought to change their beneficiary on their retirement accounts. Children are often also accidentally disinherited because the account was set up when Dad only had 2 children and never thought to add the 3rd child onto his beneficiary list.

Any accounts with designated beneficiaries gets transferred outside of probate. It is extremely important to be intentional with your beneficiary designations. Whatever the document states is what will happen to the money!

Life Insurance:
We never know when our time is up. You have to have term life insurance. Although this isn't a fun topic to talk

about, think for a moment, what would your family do if you died today? How would they pay for your funeral? What about the mortgage next month, or next year? or groceries? or college? Even for a stay at home parent, how would the family function without you? What would be the cost to replace the dozens of tasks that you complete to make the family work? Term life insurance is the number one gift to give to your family. The main risk to your family building generational wealth is when the heads of the family are unable to provide due to death.

The way term life insurance works is simple. You pay a small monthly premium, that is fixed for a set number of years, and in the unlikely event you pass away, the amount of the policy is paid out to the beneficiary on it. Term life is easy to get, it's inexpensive, and necessary. Term life is substantially more expensive for smokers than non-smokers, which says something about smoking.

At Zander Insurance, rates can be compared without giving away any personal information. Here are a few examples:

Amounts are YEARLY premiums

- 25 year old male
-     10 year $500,000 policy non smoker: $168 smoker: $620
-     20 year $500,000 policy non smoker: $240 smoker: $800
- 25 year old female
-     10 years $500,000 policy non smoker: $148 smoker: $480

- 20 year $500,000 policy non smoker: $210 smoker: $650

Although Social Security insurance provides some money for survivors, it isn't enough, especially for a stay at home parent who either has no earnings or low earnings. Term life insurance is tax free. It is highly important to name a beneficiary and to update the beneficiary information if it needs to change over time. The goal should be to have a policy that can replace your income, so having roughly 10-20X your income in coverage is necessary.

The main reason people don't get life insurance is that we tend to think that it always happens to someone else, that we are invincible. I have preached about the importance of life insurance for anyone who has kids and anyone who will listen to me. In 2014 my 21 year old sister in law passed away, she had two children ages 2 and 8 months. Now there is no amount of money in the world that would ever make up for those boys growing up without their mother, but had she had a policy, it would make the next 18 years much easier on her entire family.

Remember too that not only primary earners need life insurance. Stay at home parents also need life insurance. How much would it cost to replace all the work a stay at home mom does? Think about that before deciding against life insurance. It's inexpensive, It's easy to get and it's imperative protection to provide for your family.

Wills:

Do you have a will? If you do, is it updated? Most people

never form a legal will and those who do often don't update it even when major life events happen. Only 32% of Americans in 2020 have a will, which is down substantially from 42% in 2017. I have to admit, although I have a will, I let mine become outdated. When my wife and I first wrote our wills our children were younger, we didn't have guardianship of our nephews, we had significantly less assets, and hadn't started investing in rental real estate. We are now in the process of updating our wills.

In addition to forming a will, it is vital to revisit your will yearly to ensure it is still covering your needs. By the way, even if you have little to no assets currently, a will is still very useful. Your will also states who you want to take custody of your minor children if you pass. This is certainly not a matter you want to leave to the State.

Legacy Drawer:
Set up a Legacy drawer with all of your important documents in it. Make sure that your children and spouse know where the drawer is. This drawer should have the most recent wills, property ownership documents, life insurance documents, and investment accounts in it. There are Billions of dollars of life insurance policies that have gone unclaimed because the family didn't know they existed.

Yearly Family Meetings:

Everyone in the family should be aware of the family finances and what wills and beneficiares state and where they are located. Transparency is a major component of building generational wealth.

The Bottom Line:
Taking care of your finances will ensure that your chil-

dren will be OK. If you are in good financial health it will naturally spill over to your children. To really change your family tree the next step is to take positive intentional actions to build your children's wealth before they leave your home.

CHAPTER 12: INITIAL STEPS FOR GENERATIONAL WEALTH BUILDING

"It is not how much money you make, but how much money you keep, how hard it works for you, and how many generations you keep it for." - Robert Kiyosaki

While taking the above steps to get into a strong financial position there are several things you can do to build generational wealth that don't have any cost. It doesn't matter whether you are in debt, living paycheck to paycheck, or saving 30% of your income, you can work on these factors for yourself and your children.

Financial Education:
- Literacy: You need to have books in the home. The average middle class home has 13 age appropriate books per child. The average poor community has 1 book per 300 kids. At a minimum take your children to the library every single week without fail. Sign up for the Dolly Parton Imagination Library.

It's free and your child will receive 1 free book a month until they start school.

- Work ethic / SWEAT pledge: Take the Mike Rowe SWEAT Pledge and post it in the living room where the kids will see it every day. These principles are necessary to become wealthy. This book isn't about creating children and grandchildren who become "the idle rich", its about giving them options and a skill set to build higher than we ourselves can build.

- Be the best street sweeper. Set the example of hard work and discipline and set your ego aside. To Quote Dr. Martin Luther King Jr.

"If a man is called to be a street sweeper, he should sweep streets even as a Michaelangelo painted, or Beethoven composed music or Shakespeare wrote poetry. He should sweep streets so well that all the hosts of heaven and earth will pause to say, 'Here lived a great street sweeper who did his job well."

- Saving 20%+: Saving 10% of your income doesn't cut it. The minimum is 20%. The minimum while living under your roof is 50%. A teenager with 100% of their earnings going to wants sets them up for unrealistic expectations for the real world. It does a great disservice to young adults to have them spend 100% of their earnings on wants only to once they move out find out that the vast majority of their money has to go towards needs and very little to wants. It's no wonder our young adults do so poorly with savings.

- Avoid debt: They need to equate getting a car loan or a payday loan to be the same as going to a heroin dealer. It isn't in the realm of possibility. It just isn't a situation we go into.

- Build an emergency fund: An emergency fund keeps disasters at bay. I have seen people desperate and scared over $40. I have been desparate and scared over $40. My children will not be in that scenario. All of my kids have an established emergency fund, and your children should too. They have saved up their own emergency funds in a long term savings account at our credit union. My older teenager is approaching $1,000 and our youngest at 8 just surpassed $150. This is money they saved over time. If it took you a decade to build up your emergency fund with money you earned through hard work (and low wages), you are far less likely to let it slip through your fingers.

- Money is capital: Money can be spent, saved, given away, but it is also capital, and this is the highest use of money. Accumulation of capital is the long term game.

- Compounding interest: They need a deep understanding of how compounding interest works. Those who understand it collect it and those who don't pay it. A perfect example is the 20 year old who invests 20% of his income every year from 20 to 30 and by age 50 has $1.5 million, whereas the other 20 year old has $100,000 of student loan debt and pays $700 a month on it every single month and still owes on the loan at age 50!

- Home ownership is an advantage. Renters can

be forced to move, they don't build equity through forced savings or property appreciation. Home ownership should be a short term goal.

- Remember that "more is caught than taught" Let your kids catch you being excellent with money in your daily decisions. If you drive a $40,000 truck and always have a car payment, they will think that is normal.

- Teach them what a balance sheet is: The score card of your financial life is your balance sheet. Teaching your children what a balance sheet is and how to use it is extremely important. The visual representation of the balance sheet will give them a concrete understanding of the difference between what actions will create a millionaire and what actions will lead to poverty. The Cash Flow Game by Robert Kiyosaki is a great tool for this.

- A great practice to get into is either a monthly or quarterly family meeting where the family finances are discussed and you go over the family balance sheet and income and expenses with the kids. This breaks down the barriers of not talking about money and allows them to see the family progressing over time.

Start them a Bank Account and an Investment Account with their money:

Whether it's from Birthdays, Christmas, household chores, or odd jobs, set up each child with a piggy bank and have them split their money in 3 sections: Spend, Save, and Invest. Start them a bank account for their savings, and a Stockpile account for their investing. This is not a retirement account. It is never too early to start doing this. We started a Stockpile account for our youngest when he was 6. Compounding will allow these investments to grow to non-trivial amounts, but what really matters is building up their savings and investing muscles so that they know about investing, learn about investing and will automatically do it as a way of life as adults. This is no different than taking their shoes off to come in the house and brushing their teeth before bed. Habits.

How To Set Up An Investment Account For Your Kids Using Stockpile

Stockpile allows you to start investing with as little as $5. You can buy fractional shares, which makes entering the stock market and diversifying a lot easier. Look at Amazon as an example. Amazon stock trades at around $3,200 per share. With a traditional brokerage you would need to pay $3,200 to get into Amazon stock by buying one share. With stockpile you can buy $10 of Amazon stock if $10 is all you have to invest. Stockpile also makes it really simple to set up custodial accounts for minors. Stockpile charges 99 cent per trade; although this is inexpensive on a per trade basis, because you are buying fractional shares the total amount of money spent on acquiring 1 share can in the long run greatly exceed that of a traditional brokerage account.

Stockpile allows you to search for stocks, and you can also browse for stocks by category. To make the process easy for children they show a picture of the company's product with the stock symbol. You can also create a wishlist of stocks that you want to purchase. In addition to stocks they also have several mutual funds available. What the kids invest in is no where near as important as the fact that they are investing.

What's more important than the value of the money in the account is that an investment account changes the way children will think about money. Getting them excited about building wealth and owning companies that they consume products of is extremely important. Changing the viewpoint that money is used to buy stuff to money is used to build wealth through capital is a major turning point.

What Taxes Are Owed When Setting Up An Investment Account For Your Kids:

You might be concerned that since this is a taxable brokerage account taxes will be complicated. According to IRS publication 929 dependents can have up to $1,050 in unearned income before they have to file a tax return. Even if your children are heavily invested in high divided stocks, they would need to have over $35,000 invested with a 3% dividend yield in order to hit this number. For most families I don't think taxes will be an issue.

If your account total could exceed this while your children are minors and you want to avoid them having to file a tax return then it is imperative to invest the funds in mutual funds that pay a very low dividend. A good example is the Vanguard Mid Cap Index Fund which has a dividend yield of 1.4%. You would need to have $75,000 in this account before it would yield the $1,050 in dividends that would require your child to file a tax return.

Currently the long term capital gains rate is 0% for people in the 10% and 12% bracket. When your child becomes an adult and claims himself on his taxes he will most likely be in this bracket. It would then make sense to either sell off the positions he has (after not buying any new stock in the account for 1 year) and then re-investing that money in a Roth IRA.

Encourage Them To Start A Micro Business:
Perhaps pooled Christmas gifts with grandparents could be seed money. I've read stories about a kid who started a candy stand in her front yard, a young man mows lawns, and another kid who uses a 3d printer to sell face mask ear savers on eBay. Aside from the money, the education these kids will get from running a micro business is invaluable.

Have Them Work While In High School:

You also must set guidelines for saving and investing. Working while going to school 20 hrs per week during the school year at $10 per hour is $10,000 per year.

Investing earnings is a requirement. For a 16 year old who has 50 years before the standard retirement age, there is a TON of time for compounding interest to work its magic. Set them up a ROTH IRA to invest their earnings in and insist that they put at least 50% of their earnings into investing.

Job Seeking Assistance:
I think this is highly overlooked in our society. Helping our kids find the right job for them is key to getting ahead. I spent 3 years working for right around minimum wage because the employer worked around my school schedule. In retrospect I bet I could have found a job paying twice as much per hour had I looked diligently that I could have built my school schedule around. I will put in a lot of effort into helping my kids develop skills and find jobs that are higher paying, especially when starting out.

Apply For Scholarships As A Job:
There are over 750,000 scholarships out there that your child can earn, with total yearly payouts of over $1 billion. Not all scholarships are full ride scholarships reserved for stellar athletes and valedictorians. There are thousands of scholarships available ranging from a few hundred dollars to tens of thousands of dollars.

Applying for scholarships en masse every day for months on end will result in some wins. Focusing on lower dollar scholarships and scholarships that require essays is a great way to increase your odds since fewer people are applying for them. I recently watched a TikTok of a young lady who applied for, and won a scholarship, upon winning she found out that their were 12 scholarships available and only 9 people applied. The more shots you take, the more likely you are to win.

Most scholarships require you to fill out a FAFSA form for financial aid, so make sure this is also in on time every year.

Let Your Kids Live At Home:
Letting them stay at home while they are working full time keeps them from having all the normal expenses of rent, utilities, groceries, etc. Living at home for 2 years they should be able to save well over 50% of their pay at little incremental cost to you. This is the easiest method to give your child a head start in life without dipping into your income or savings.

This removes the spending on needs, which should allow them to invest 100% of the money that otherwise would be going to needs.

If your child is working full time 40 hours a week and

earning $12 per hour, if he saves 50% of his pay he will save $25,000 in 2 years. Starting out with $25,000 is life changing. That's a full emergency fund and a down payment for a house! Let your children stay at home, but ensure you are having weekly discussions on their income, expenses, time management, and investments. A monthly meeting to go over their balance sheet is required in exchange for them living at home rent free.

The best part? Implementing all of these solutions didn't cost you anything.

CHAPTER 13: HIGHER EDUCATION

"We are lending money we don't have to kids who can't pay it back to train them for jobs that no longer exist. That's nuts." -Mike Rowe

Planning and paying for college is a major undertaking for most families. I believe strongly that further education is important to our success as individuals and as a society. Further education does not necessarily mean a 4 year bachelors degree for a desk job.

I also encourage everyone to learn about Mike Rowe's SWEAT Pledge. It is vitally important to have detailed, meaningful conversations with our children and other young adults in our lives to help steer them in a mindful direction. The mistakes that can be made in this arena are too costly to just stand by and watch. With planning and hard work I graduated with a Bachelor's degree for under $13,000.

Our children need to plan for what they want to do.

Maybe college isn't the right path. Explore other options such as trade schools, apprenticeships, or starting their own businesses. I know a guy who started a snow removal company in high school who started out with just his labor and a shovel. Today he has several trucks and employees and works year round, expanding into lawn care, landscaping, and hauling.

Trade schools and apprenticeship programs are a great option. Many skilled trades are already severely understaffed with an aging work force. These programs pay the apprentices while they are learning on the job, include great benefits, and many skilled tradesperson can earn into the six figures as Journeymen. Absolutely have your children consider skilled trades such as welders, electricians, millwrights, carpenters, boilermakers, lineman, and various other skilled trades. Many skilled trades workers go on to eventually start their own businesses based around their trades.

Starting as young as 9th grade, have them make a plan regarding where they want to go to school and what for. This plan needs to be researched, and include knowing the demand for college grads in this field, the costs associated with the schools they want to go to, and a plan for paying for college. Then the young adult can compare these costs and benefits to other options, and find the best deal. In order to get a penny from the bank of mom and dad, there has to be a serious proposal that shows an understanding of costs and benefits associated with the degree.

As an example, if Junior wants to go to an out of state private school to earn a communications degree that costs $150K, for a job that earns $30K a year, he needs to learn that that doesn't make sense. Having him run the numbers will teach him that. There are many skilled trades that require a 1 year certificate or 2 year degree program that offer great career tracks and are in high demand, from plastics, to welding, to nursing, there are several other routes to gain education and increase wages than a 4 year degree. My local community college has a three week program to teach truck driving, which prepares students to get their Class A license. The program costs just over $4,000 and they have employers beating down the door to pay graduates over $1,000 a week.

Drastically Reducing The Financial Burden Of Paying For College:

In -State public schools only:
The first method is to insist that out of state and private schools are off the table. For the vast majority of two year and four year degrees the payback is just not there.

Two years of community college:
The tuition and fees are substantially less expensive and the opportunity exists to live at home, rather than on campus, saving thousands. After transferring to a four year school, the final institution is all that appears on the degree. So if Junior does two years at community college, saving over $35,000, his final degree only states "Graduate, Michigan State University."

There may also be an opportunity for your kids to earn an associates degree while still in high school. A new program in my county focused on our community college allows students to graduate with an associates degree and high school at the same time by taking college courses in their junior and senior year, then delaying high school graduation for a 5th year and attending college courses during this time.

The best part? The cost to the student is $0! A similar program is being proposed on the national level.

Room and Board:
The cost of living in a double dorm room at my closest state school ends up being $595.50 per month based on a 4 month, 16 week semester. Looking at the housing ads on craigslist I found dozens of listings for between $300 and $350 per month. Many of these locations are close to school, have washer and dryers, and full kitchens. Renting a room in a large house like this is far more cost effective. A $350 per month rental cuts room and board per year from $4,800 to $2,800 per year, saving $2,000 per year, or $4,000 over a two year degree.

Food Costs:
We have already started teaching our kids how to grocery shop competitively. One of the reasons kids in dorm rooms need to have a meal plan is because dorm rooms don't have kitchens. By purchasing groceries and utilizing the kitchen in a rented house students can save a fortune. It is entirely possible for a college kid to eat well on under $50 a week. This brings food costs over a 16 week semester to $800 or $1,600 for a year. This saves another $2,650 per year, or $5,300 over two years.

Scholarships:
Scholarships are a great way to cover some college expenses. The majority of scholarships do require financial need be demonstrated. Many are for specific majors, and will require essays to be considered. Scholarships that are school specific (and for smaller schools), relatively low amounts, and require essays are applied for by fewer total students, so that is where to apply, rather than for large national scholarships, where the odds of winning are lower. Have your child apply

for scholarships like it's a full time job.

CLEP exams:
CLEP exams allow students to essentially 'test out' of a class. CLEP exams cost around $100 and the credits gained from them can range from 3 credits up to 16 credits, depending on the exam, the school being attended and the score received. CLEP exams are great for basic courses and for electives.

5 CLEP exams at $100 each (assuming paying $20 for a study guide) is $500. 15 credits at a community college is $1,965, not including any books or room and board fees. That's $1,500 of money in real savings. Coupled with prudent use of the American Opportunity Tax Credit and you could be looking at an associates degree costing only a couple grand.

The savings are much larger at a four year school. At Michigan State University costs are $480 per credit hour. For a student who chose to attend a four year school instead of transferring over would save around $7,200 on tuition, plus another $4,400 on room and board for a total savings of $11,600!

Methods For Paying For College :
Beyond saving money by using the thrifty ideas above, here are some methods to cover the remainder of the college costs.

Working:
This is the starting point. There is nothing wrong with requiring children to work during the school year and during college. Working 20 hours a week at a $10 per hour job during the school year, and 40 hours at $10 per hour during the

summer equals roughly $12,500. I repeat: There is nothing wrong with young adults working and paying for college out of their earnings. It won't cover everything, but it will make a large dent.

Financial Aid:
Fill out the FAFSA form completely and accurately. The FAFSA calculation for "financial need" is overly complex, but understanding it and properly responding and planning for this incentive will result in a significant difference in college costs. The maximum pell grant that anyone can receive is $6,345 per year, for a maximum of 12 semesters lifetime. While the calculations for a Pell grant are complicated, there are several estimator tools online.

Some basics of Pell Grant eligibility: The government determines what the estimated family contribution to education should be, based on family size, income and assets of the parents, and income and assets of the students. Retirement accounts and home equity on a primary residence do not count towards asset tests. $38,500 of other assets are exempt from the asset test as well. Even if you are certain your family will not qualify for financial aid, it is still important to file the FAFSA because many scholarships require you to do so in order to be eligible.

Tax incentives:
The American Opportunity Tax Credit can be claimed for 4 years, per student for a maximum of $2,500 per year. The first $2,000 of eligible expenses receives a $1 for $1 tax credit. The next $2,000 receives a 25 cent for $1 tax credit. 40% of this credit is refundable, so even if no tax liability is owed, the credit holds an advantage. There are income limits on this credit. This tax credit alone, used for 2 years of full time study at a local community college covers 62%

of the cost. If you spread 60 credits out over 3 years at 20 credits a year, it would cover 82% of the cost, with 1 year of credit remaining. This means each year the student would only have to pay a net of $500 per year, for 3 years. This strategy works best for a student who is only planning on earning a 2 year degree, for those planning on earning a four year degree it makes sense to get the full credit each year, by attending full time, incurring total costs of $4,000 for 4 years to maximize the credit. Using this credit as part of a college payment strategy can result in a free associates degree.

National Guard/Military:
One of the driving reasons to join the military is the excellent benefits that are offered, the most notable being the GI Bill, which can cover 100% of all tuition and fees for 4 years of in state public school, or a maximum of $25,162 per academic year for private or foreign schools. Additionally, the GI Bill may provide housing assistance while attending school.

Promise Zones:
In Michigan we have several school districts that are in promise zones, Benton Harbor school district, which includes charter schools in the area, is in a promise zone. This particular promise zone guarantees to fully cover 2 years of community college. The student must apply for financial aid, and any amount that is not covered by a federal Pell Grant will be paid by the promise zone, which is funded through donors and tax increment financing. Not only does this cover those first two years, it allows for 4 more years to be claimed on the American Opportunity Tax Credit, since the first two years expenses are covered. It is possible to take an extra semester to graduate to get a $2500 credit for 3 years.

Dual Enrolment/Early College:
Many high schools have partnerships with community colleges to help give students a head start. High schools will often pay for the tuition and fees for these courses, and students can take courses that satisfy both high school requirements and college requirements, allowing them the opportunity to go as far as finishing an associates degree while in high school, at little to no cost to the parents.

Parental Cash Flow And Savings:
There are a couple decent tools for saving for college, coverdale education savings accounts (ESA), and 529 plans. A coverdale account works like a Roth IRA. Contributions of up to $2,000 a year are non-deductible, but withdrawals for education expenses are tax free. Withdrawals from these accounts can be used by a student in the same year as the American Opportunity Tax Credit, or the Lifetime Learning Tax Credit, but not for the same expense. Example: Your child has $6,000 of college expenses. The first $4,000 receives the American opportunity tax credit ($2,500) and then fund the remaining $2,000 from the ESA. Money can only be added to the account until the beneficiary is 18, and at age 30, distributions must be made.

529 plans are state sponsored, tax advantaged plans for college savings. 529 plans are viewed as owner controlled, not beneficiary controlled. Every state's 529 plan may be different, but one advantage to this is that you can use any state's 529 plan, not just the state in which you reside or plan to have a child attend college. Money is put in after taxes, like an ESA, and can be withdrawn tax free for qualified expenses. 529 plans allow for much larger sums of money to be put away than an ESA. 529 plan beneficiaries can be changed, so if an older child decides not to go to school, the beneficiary can be changed to his younger siblings or to his future children.

"Graduating college with large student loans versus with parents footing the bill is the difference between starting a family and career with debts versus lack of debts. It also is the difference between needing to pay off this debt monthly versus saving money. And it is the difference between mortgage lenders looking at a credit record already saddled with large monthly obligations versus few obligations." - Thomas M. Shapiro The Hidden Cost of Being African American

Working hard to keep college costs as low as possible for your children, taking advantage of scholarships, grants, and financial aid, and chipping in some money is highly important to starting your children off on the right foot.

CHAPTER 14: BUILDING GENERATIONAL WEALTH WITH YOUR SAVINGS

Instead of trying to build a brick wall, lay a brick everyday. Eventually you'll look up and you'll have a brick wall. - Nipsey Hussle

How do you eat an elephant? One bite at a time. You don't need a million dollars or a six figure income to start planting seeds for your children's future. Once you are in a position to utilize some of your savings towards building generational wealth, follow these steps:

Using Tax Refunds to Build Generational Wealth:
You know that $2,000 tax credit you get per kid? It was only $1,000 only a few years ago. Use half of the increase, $500 per kid per year to invest for your child. No matter what age they are you can start an easy to use UGMA (Uniform Gift To Minors Act) investment account. I use Stock-

pile for my kids. $500 per year for only 10 years at 10% growth will become $1 million after 60 years. Congress recently increased this tax credit to $3,000 and to $3,600 for children under 6. Consider investing some or all of this increase for your child as well.

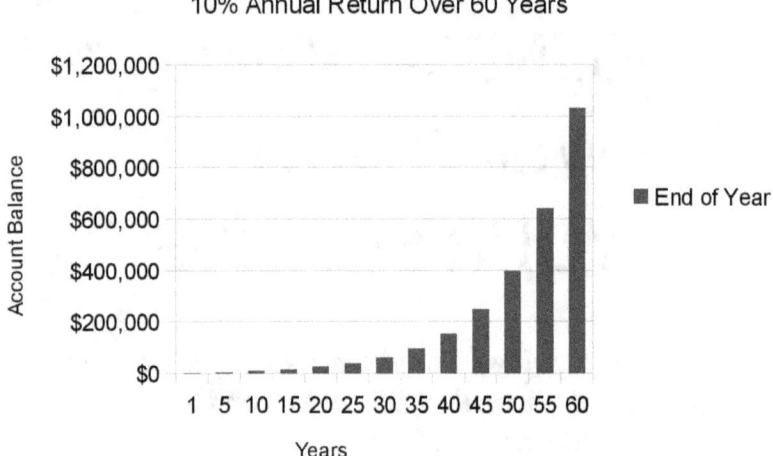

Weekly Gift of $10 (or more):

Along the same line as using tax refunds to fund UGMA accounts, do a weekly gift of $10 per week into their UGMA accounts. Most people of any income level can come up with $10 a week. $520 a year. Coupled with the $500 a year from the child tax credit, the total of $1,020 a year, or $85 a month invested at 8% over 18 years will grow to $41,000 by the time they are 18. I use the same Stockpile account that our kids contribute their investing money into for this.

Roth IRAs and Matching Funds:

Once your children have earned income they can contribute to a Roth IRA, up to $6,000 a year or the total of their earned income, whichever is less. With a Roth IRA money is put in after taxes are already paid on it (and a teen usually has very low taxes, if any) and then it grows tax free forever and the money can be withdrawn tax free after 59 ½, or at any time before that for a first time home purchase.

Match their retirement account like an employer to get them excited about saving for retirement. You can put a max on it that's lower than the federal max (Which is $6,000 or 100% of earned income, whichever is less). You can match $1 for $1, or if that currently isn't feasible, you could do 50 cents or a quarter on the dollar. Alternatively you could go the other route and match 2 to 1 or 3 to 1. The main point is to get them started and to know that it's important to save and invest and that compounding interest is the 8th wonder of the world. If your match would put them over the maximum Roth IRA amount, you can put the remainder of your match into their Stockpile UGMA (Uniform Gift To Minors) account.

It is possible to speed up their first job too. Most employers require workers to be 16 to start, however a child can be self employed at any age. Rather than waiting until they can work at McDonalds at 16, Have them start a simple lawn care or babysitting business at 12. or a toy resale business at 10. Self employment income counts. Now they will have to pay self employment taxes of 15.2%, but that is well worth it. A great option is if you are in the position to cover this, credit the money they would pay in taxes back to them.

As an example, if Sean earns $3,000 ($30 per lawn 5 lawns, 20 mows per season) doing lawn care throughout the year, and files a tax return, he would owe no federal income taxes, but would owe Self employment taxes of $456. Sean needs to be able to spend some of his money, perhaps 25%. He is still allowed to contribute up to $3,000 to his Roth IRA. If he spends $600 and owed taxes of $456, then he has $1,944 to invest in his Roth IRA, not bad!

Here's where matching comes in. Offer to match 1:1 his contributions. If he puts in $1,500 you put in $1,500. Alternatively this match can be scaled up our down based on your situation. If you can afford to help more, offer a 2:1 match and put in $2,000 if he puts in $1,000. If you can only afford $500 offer a 25% match, if he puts in $2,000 you will put in $500. Keep in mind that for a 12 year old, by the time he is 65 any money he invests now at 8% average returns will grow to about 68 times as much. A $500 contribution will turn into $34,000! If he averaged 10% returns it would grow to 196 times the original amount, $500 would become $98,000.

Beyond the actual value his investment and your matching funds will grow into the real value being earned here is the lesson that work = money, and that money is used to build capital. Instilling this at an early age will turn your child into a lifelong hard worker, saver and investor. If he can save over half his income at 12, he will be a rockstar saver at 25.

401K Contributions: If their job offers a 401K match ensure that they go for this and offer to double match this into their IRA. Not only will they get the free money from the employer, but they may also qualify for the retirement savers tax credit which can be up to $1,000.

Life Insurance:
I have a large amount of life insurance that goes to my wife If I die. If we both die my sister in law is the bene-

ficiary of a large chunk of money to care for our children, and the rest is split evenly between our kids. Each would have enough money if I died if left invested would make them multimillionaires at retirement age. For non smokers life insurance is extremely cheap. I had kids young however I plan to maintain life insurance policies for several decades because it is so cheap and can give my heirs a major boost.

I plan to pay for life insurance policies for all of our children once they become adults. I want to get them a 20 year policy that is in place before they have any significant health issues that could cause denial or before they start a family so that it doesn't become something that falls on the back burner. Many people put off getting life insurance as a minor administrative task and sometimes it's too late. I personally know several young adults who have died unexpectedly without life insurance. The death of our children isn't something we want to think about, but it is imperative to ensure their future family will be protected.

A 20 year term policy for an 18 year old non smoker is incredibly inexpensive. The beneficiary of the policy until they have a spouse or children can be left blank, going to their estate. This way when they do have a spouse or children the money will still go to them, regardless of if the policy beneficiary is updated.

First Home Purchase:
Offer to give down payment assistance with a first time home purchase. If they want to put down 20%, but only have 10% saved up, match their down payment to get them into the loan. If they have the 20% let them buy the house then throw the equivalent of 20% of the home value on the mortgage. This would drop their 15 year mortgage to just over a 10 year mortgage. On a 30 year it

would drop it to just over 19 years.

Even better, if you have become a real estate investor, buy a house with them and fix it up with them. Donate your labor towards the rehab, and don't make a profit on the deal. They end up with a $60,000 home that only cost $30,000 and learn a ton on the project. Go a step further and encourage them to buy a duplex or a fourplex to get started on rental income.

Leave An Inheritance While You Are Alive

Launching into adulthood is a crazy expensive time period. Typically in the first decade of adulthood we attend secondary education, get married, have children, buy a house, and start to save for retirement. This is a ton of expensive items all at once. The one item that falls to the wayside is typically saving for retirement, which is where real wealth can be built. Providing help at this stage of the game is much more important than leaving a large inheritance upon your death, especially if you are a young parent. My stepson was born when I was 17. It's highly probable that by the time I die he will be a senior citizen and long since retired. Him receiving a million bucks from me when he is 70 is nowhere near as helpful as receiving tens of thousands of dollars of help in his 20s or 30s.

CHAPTER 15: START INVESTING IN RENTAL PROPERTIES

The key to financial freedom and great wealth is a person's ability to convert earned income into passive and/or portfolio income. - Robert Kiyosaki

I love rental real estate for building my personal wealth, but it is also a great way to build generational wealth for your children and grandchildren. The real estate I buy is value real estate. Typically the houses I buy pay for themselves in 5 years. That's a 20% cap rate.

After your tenants have paid off your rental property you could give it to your child. If you bought houses with similar profit potential as the ones I buy, you could rent it out for 4 to 5 years and reinvest all the money in paying it down. After 5 years the house is paid off and you could give it to your child.

If outright giving a house to your child doesn't sit well with you, you could at a minimum seller finance it to them at very favorable terms, such as selling it at your buy cost rather than the current market rate, and financing over a shorter term with little to no down payment.

A house that would appraise at $64,000 would typically require a 5% down payment of $3,200, closing costs of around $3,000 and on a 30 year mortgage would come with a $290 a month payment and cost $43,700 in interest over the life of the loan.

Selling that same house to your child for $32,000 with 5% down would require a $1,600 down payment and closing costs would be only a few hundred dollars since no bank is involved. A 10 year mortgage at 3% would have the same $290 a month payment, and only cost $4,825 in interest over the life of the loan.

This is a house that you already own free and clear, that the tenants paid off, and now you can get all your money back, with interest, while also taking 20 years off your child's mortgage and reducing the cost to get into home ownership from $6,200 to $1,600.

Real Life Example:
We use what's called the BRRRR method to buy our rental properties. BRRRR stands for Buy, Rehab, Rent, Refinance, Repeat. We used a Home Equity Line of Credit (Heloc) on our primary residence to buy a 3 bedroom house for $24,000 plus $500 in closing costs and $8,500 for the rehab. 6 months after the purchase the house appraised at $64,000. A 75% loan to value $48,000 loan pays for the $3,000 closing costs on the loan, and pays back $33,000 on the heloc, plus $12,000 in cash. We kept the cash as an extra emergency fund for our rental property business, however you could get a loan for $36,000 instead to break even. The important point is that we have $0 of our cash tied up in this house and are free to

shop for the next one.

The house rents at $900 per month. We pay $84 in property taxes, $32 in insurance, $40 for maintenance, and on a $36,000 3.5% 15 year mortgage we would pay $98 in mortgage interest and $156 in principal. This property would cash flow $490 a month. By putting the extra cash flow on the mortgage each month, this property would pay itself off in 53 months, just under 4.5 years. The whole time, $0 of our cash was actually in the property. After the refinance the bank had lent 100% of our cost, and the tenants will pay the property off.

Rental Real Estate Real Life Example				
Purchase Price	$24,000	Rent	$900
Closing Costs	$580	Property Taxes	-$84
Rehab Costs	$7,602	Insurance	-$32
Carrying Costs	$846	Maintenance	-$40
Total Invested	$33,028	Mortgage Interest	-$98
		Depreciation	-$74
Appraisal	$64,000		
Total Value Added	$30,972	Net Income	$572
Total Invested	$33,028	Mortgage Principal	-$156
Closing Costs	$3,046	Cash Flow	$490
Total Loan	$36,074		
Cash In Property	$0	Months to pay off	53

Do one of these for each child. If it takes 7 years to pay off the house it is still worth doing. You ultimately had no cash come out of your pocket and your tenants paid for a house for your child. If your child is not 18 yet or not ready to own a home yet keep the rental and use the proceeds to invest in their stockpile account or Roth IRA. This of course doesn't have to end with 1 house per child, you can keep recycling the initial cash every 6 months, since the banks tend to require a 6 month waiting period to do a cash out refinance. If you buy a house every 6 months, or even 1 house a year that has similar numbers to the example above it won't take long to build serious long term generational wealth.

Self Managing Vs. Professionally Managed:

Currently my wife and I self manage all of our properties. There are some advantages and disadvantages to going with a property manager. If you have a very demanding W2 job, a property manager is probably the better option. Angie no longer works and my job is seasonally for about half the year, so we have the time available to self manage.

The main driver for choosing to self manage is the difference in incentives for an owner and for a property manager. The owner's goal is to maximize the income from his asset. The property managers goal is to minimize the time he spends on each individual property. Property managers are more likely to under price your units. By pricing a house $200 less than the going market rate they will get dozens of applications, immediately, and whoever gets the house will keep complaints to a minimum because they have a really good deal. This also leads us to having more deferred maintenance.

Another downside to professional management is that they are notorious for over charging on repairs. Now, I'm not saying ALL property managers do this, but it is a prevalent practice. As an example, let's say a tenant has a running toilet. If you were to fix it yourself, it would likely take 10 minutes of time and cost less than $20 to change out the guts in the toilet. The property manager will send their maintenance guy who they will bill out at $50 an hour. They will charge 2 hours for the service call and $50 for supplies. $150 vs. $20.

That's the downside, but there is of course a very real upside to hiring out property management. Rather than buying yourself a part time job with each house, you are truly buying an asset. So what if you give up 25% of your profit to the manager, you are able to scale to a lot more houses if someone else is taking care of everything. You don't get a call when something's wrong with the house. You don't have to vet tenants, deal with evictions, or any of that other nonsense. The property manager does that.

Keeping Costs Low:

Buying the house: We buy bank repossession houses with several "unknowns". These houses don't qualify for financing and need substantial work. Typically we don't make an offer unless the house has sat on the market for over 30 days. We are not emotionally attached, and neither is the bank. We can typically get around a 30% discount off of true market value this way.

Appealing Property Tax Assessments: Properties are often over assessed. In Michigan there is a formal process for appealing the assessment on your home. It is a one page form to fill out. I typically include recent comparable sales, as well as my purchase agreement when appealing my property taxes. I will also compare my assessment to the assessment of similar houses in the area. So far I have won 5 out of 6 property tax appeals.

Property Insurance: Having multiple houses gives you a good multi-policy discount. We also keep a $2,000 deductible on each house. Our average rental insurance premium is $35 a month.

CHAPTER 16: START A SMALL BUSINESS

> *"There is only one way to make money: finding out what other people want or need and then providing those things to as many of our fellow humans as possible. This is the only way to earn money, no matter your occupation." "money is the consequence of working, not the goal."* -Rabbi Lapin

My wife and I have started buying used books at thrift stores and yard sales and reselling on Amazon. I also operate the blog Action Econ and have written this book. We are using a large percentage of these side hustles to build generational wealth. We all have 168 hours a week. Spending 5 to 10 extra hours a week building a small business can change your family tree even if the amounts are really small. Invest the earnings as they come in and have a plan to involve the kids in the business so they can add value and take over parts of it when they are ready.

Business Structure:

When starting out most people will open a small business as a sole proprietorship. You own 100% of the business and report the business income on Schedule C of your 1040 tax return. The net earnings of the business are taxed at your marginal federal tax rate like ordinary earned income and you will also have to pay 15.2% self employment tax.

Starting a business doesn't have to be big. You don't need a physical store or to spend a ton of money to get started. Any activity that generates profits is a business. Starting a family business does three important things. First of all it stops you from being 100% dependent on a W2 job for your livelihood. This diversification of income is very important for any family and can help weather the storm of a job loss or reduction in hours.

Secondly, you are building an opportunity for your children to earn money and potentially have their own careers inside the business, rather than having to work a job for someone else. This is especially critical for when they are first entering the workforce and opportunities are scarce. Having your children work in your small business helps develop their work ethic and build invaluable skills for the workplace. A child that works 500 hours a year in their parents business for 10 years before turning 18 has a heck of an advantage over a child who turns 18 and has never worked a day in their lives.

The third and final important benefit of starting your own business is that it allows you the opportunity to put more money towards generational wealth building. By having more total family cash flow from the business you can put more money into your child's UGMA account, and/or through their earnings working for the business they can fund their own Roth IRA.

Hiring Your Children:

You can hire your children to work in your business by filing for an Employer Identification Number (EIN) and filing an I-9 form with the IRS.

Hiring your children has some substantial advantages. The act of officially hiring your child as an employee greatly reduces the family tax burden. As an example, let's say with your total income your marginal federal tax rate is 25%. With a state tax rate of 4% and self employment tax of 15.2%, your total effective tax rate on any business income is 44.2%. This is really high.

If your business earns $30,000 this means you will pay $13,260 in taxes on that income. Here's where hiring your children comes in. Let's say you have two children and they can contribute substantial efforts towards the business. This is great because it frees up your time, which is already in high demand with your day job.

If you have two children and pay them each $12,500 for their efforts over the course of the year, you will reduce your business income on your taxes from $30,000 to $5,000, reducing your tax bill to $2,210. Because your children's earnings are under the total standard deduction, which is $12,550, they will not owe any federal income tax, and since they are your children and under the age of 18, they don't have to pay payroll taxes either. Their tax bills are $0 each, they would only have to pay state income taxes. We reduced your taxes by $11,050, gave your children the tools to earn their own money, and they paid no taxes! This benefit is magnified the higher your tax rate is. For a high income family in a high income tax state the tax savings is closer to 60% than 45%.

Now, because they have actual earnings, they can contribute $6,000 to fully fund a Roth IRA. You can open a custodial Roth IRA at any brokerage firm like Vanguard or Fidelity for your minor child. Your business doesn't have to grow to a profit of $30,000 a year for this to make sense. The numbers still work well if the business is earning $10,000 a year. Have each kid earn $3,000. This is still way better than not starting a business, and they can still contribute up to $3,000 to their Roth IRAs.

The best part? Child labor laws largely don't apply to your children working in your business. You can hire your 6 year old in your business and pay him wages as a W2 employee. You can hire your children a full decade before anyone else can. As we learned in earlier chapters, starting earlier exponentially increases the total wealth we can build.

Your child has to be doing actual work in the business and at a rate that would be normal in the market place. You also need to keep records of hours worked and earnings. Essentially, you can't pay your 3 year old $100 an hour to be a marketing manager. You could pay your 6 year old $12 an hour as a general laborer to move books in and out of the house, clean them, and sort them. It has to make sense and be defensible if the IRS asks questions.

From a documentation standpoint it helps to contract payroll through a company like ADP to strengthen the paper trail of the money. Add in automatic deposits to the child's bank account and automatic contributions from the bank account to their custodial Roth IRA to provide an excellent accounting defense of what you are doing if audited by the IRS and to automatically build wealth for your kids.

The compounding interest numbers get really interesting when you do this. For a child that starts investing $6,000 in their Roth IRA at age 6 with compounded returns of 10% annually, by age 18 they will have $138,000. If they never contribute any more money, by 55 they will have $5.5 million!

I can't stress enough how big of a deal this is. Getting your children earning money and investing in tax protected accounts over a decade before they would normally be eligible and two decades before most of their peers start investing is an amazing head start. The best part of it is that you aren't giving them the money to invest, they have to earn it! You are only setting up the system that makes their earnings possible.

Start A Big Family Business:
If your small business grows to the point where it can be a full time job for a few people and is continuing to grow, then set up a family LLC. This allows you to give away ownership in the business. This is the strategy Sam Walton used to pass down wealth to his children tax free. In 1953 when the Waltons owned only a few small five and dime stores Walton Enterprises LLC was formed with all four Walton children and Sam and Helen Walton all owning 20% stakes in the company. In his book "Made In America" Sam stated

> "The best way to reduce paying estate taxes is to give your assets away before they appreciate." - Sam Walton

Sam Walton got all the notoriety for becoming the richest man in the world, but the truth of the matter was he only owned 20% of what was being reported. Walton Enterprises not only owned and operated all the Walmart stores, it also invested in banks, newspapers, and any other investments that the family was interested in. Today between Walton Enterprises and the Walton Family Foundation the Walton's control 50% of the company, which is unheard of for a company that has been public for 50 years. This is actually a 12% increase in ownership since Sam published "Made In America" in 1992.

This structure requires the family to decide together on how to spend money and what direction to go in with the business. It allows the children and subsequent grandchildren to hold ownership with the management of the shares / investments done together. No one individual can decide to sell shares or dilute the ownership. This keeps majority ownership with the family and potentially protects rogue children from squandering wealth. All they would get from the business is the same dividend anyone else would get...golden eggs, not the goose.

If a business (or any other investment) is held in an LLC, you can give away shares of ownership in the LLC to your children or grandchildren at present value, up to the $15,000 per person per year maximum without filing for gift tax. Consult a tax attorney for this setup. Since you can do this in an ongoing fashion every year, you not only transfer ownership of the assets without incurring any debt or tax liabilities, you also start syphoning off some income to your children during this time. If say over the first 10 years you transfer 25% of the ownership to your children and the LLC has $100,000 of income, $75,000 would stay with you and $25,000 would go to the children.

Another trick with this method is that the shares going to the children and grandchildren can be discounted because they are not given voting rights and because they can't sell their shares on the open market. This is beneficial if your business has become extremely successful and is growing faster than what you can give away each year without tax implications. So if the total value of the LLC is $1 million rather than giving 1.5% per year to each person at a face value of $15,000 you could give them closer to 2.5% per year or $25,000. Granted, this won't apply to most people, but it is an interesting way to work around the estate tax laws.

This strategy kills 4 birds with 1 stone. It transfers assets to your heirs avoiding the estate tax. It gives away assets before they appreciate, allowing your children and grandchildren to receive asset appreciation early on and further reduce your future taxable estate. It transfers income to your children and grandchildren to give them passive income now (which they can re-invest into their own retirement accounts or rental properties), and it reduces your taxable income in the highest bracket for the year.

CHAPTER 17: GRANDCHILDREN AND GREAT GRANDCHILDREN

My grandchildren will be eating from the moves I make this decade" - Xavier C Miller

By getting your money right and helping out your children, your grandchildren will start out life with a vastly different trajectory than you did or your children did. By the time grandchildren are born you may be in a more financially stable position AND your children should also be in a more financially stable position.

When my grandchildren are born I want to give them their inheritance. Each grandchild will receive the same amount of money, which will be $16,000. $8,000 from me, and $8,000 from my wife. This money will be placed in a taxable brokerage account with their parents as the guardian until they are 18 years old. The money will be invested primarily in a Mid-Cap Growth index fund, which gives off very little dividends so that while minors they should not have to file a tax return. Building generational wealth is much easier when you start at birth rather than starting in their 50s or 60s.

$16,000 at 8% annualized returns will be $60,000 at 18, $700,000 at 50, and $1 Million at age 55. Effectively I am funding their retirement. In Chapter 1 we talked about compounding interest and doubling periods. The goal is to reduce the amount of doubling periods needed to become wealthy. By giving them $16,000 we are eliminating 4 out of 10 doubling periods on the way to $1 million and gaining 2 doubling periods by starting at birth instead of at 20. By starting at birth we are also giving them a 50 – 60 year time horizon for needing the money.

But Wait, All These Capital Gains Are Taxable!!

Yes, they are, and we want to avoid paying tax as much as possible.

Currently long term capital gains are taxed at a 0% rate as long as the tax filer is in the 10% or 12% tax bracket. Currently this would be single filers with a taxable income of $40,525 or below. When adding in the standard deduction, this results in an AGI of $53,075. For married filers the amounts are doubled.

There is also a "kiddie tax" on unearned income. Essentially, the first $1,000 of unearned income is tax free, the 2nd $1,000 is taxed at the dependent's tax rate, and anything over $2,000 is taxed at the parents tax rate. Because of this we don't want to harvest capital gains until the grandchild is either 25 or is able to claim himself as a non-dependent filer.

Most likely the children will become non-dependents at age 18 by earning enough money to provide for over half their own support. During these years it would make sense to harvest as many capital gains as possible by selling the assets in this account, up until they have emptied the account and repurchased new investments, now with a new cost basis equal to the total value in the account, rather than $16,000. They will pay no capital gains taxes on doing this. Building generational wealth is much easier when you know the tax laws and take action to avoid overpaying on taxes.

As an example:

It reasonably costs around $12,000 per year to support a person. If at age 18 these kids work 1200 hours at $10 per hour they would hit this threshold. Now they can claim themselves as non-dependents.

Now, they can sell assets and take long term capital gains of $41,075 per year (maxing out the 12% tax bracket). They should then immediately re-invest the proceeds into their own Roth IRA to the max, and into their own taxable account. After 2 years the account that I funded is empty.

Now at age 20 they have roughly $12,000 in a Roth IRA that will never be taxed and $64,000 in a taxable account with a tax basis of $64,000. Since this is all "new money" now, it is much easier to deal with. They can either keep it in the taxable account, or as time goes on filter this money into their IRAs and 401Ks. They would pay zero taxes on all the gains made from my initial investment.

To filter this money into a workplace 401K, they simply would need to increase their 401K contribution at work to hit the maximum allowed and invest it in a similar mutual fund. Then withdrawal the equivalent funds from their taxable account to live on, tax free.

Won't Inflation make all these amounts worth much less?

I've already accounted for inflation in these calculations. The 8% returns I am using are assuming 10% actual returns and 2% yearly inflation.

I decided to check these estimates through analyzing historical situations. I ran scenarios for what would happen with a lump sum invested in 10 year increments starting in 1930. To figure this out I first used calculator.net's CPI calculator to find the inflation adjusted equivalent in all of these years for $16,000.

I then found an investment calculator that figured out what a 100% stock investment allocation would yield in 10 year spans. This is following the IFA 100 Index portfolio. I then created a second column comparing those numbers with inflation adjusted numbers, using the same inflation calculator. Here is the resulting spreadsheet:

JOHN CRABTREE

Start Year	Inflation Adj. 16K in 2020	10 years Nominal	10 years 2020	20 years Nominal	20 years 2020	30 years Nominal	30 years 2020
1930	$1,066	$904	$16,703	$3,275	$35,235	$16,091	$141,340
1940	$866	$3,034	$32,642	$14,909	$130,958	$43,829	$305,904
1950	$1,487	$7,596	$66,722	$22,329	$155,845	$76,399	$269,571
1960	$1,822	$5,115	$35,700	$17,501	$61,752	$105,513	$217,760
1970	$2,292	$7,627	$26,911	$45,984	$94,903	$151,414	$232,503
1980	$4,535	$29,210	$60,284	$96,182	$147,692	$185,776	$221,387
1990	$7,752	$24,367	$37,417	$47,065	$56,087	$112,598	$112,598
2000	$10,420	$19,539	$23,284	$46,745	$46,745		
2010	$13,426	$31,060	$31,060				
Goal			$32,000		$64,000		$128,000

Start Year	Inflation Adj. 16K in 2020	40 years Nominal	40 years 2020	50 years Nominal	50 years 2020	60 years Nominal	60 years 2020
1930	$1,066	$47,033	$328,266	$161,844	$571,060	$977,475	$2,017,329
1940	$866	$149,959	$529,125	$905,401	$1,868,581	$3,029,162	$4,651,416
1950	$1,487	$460,611	$950,617	$1,526,169	$2,343,502	$3,014,335	$3,592,151
1960	$1,822	$347,424	$533,485	$672,439	$801,338	$1,626,121	$1,626,121
1970	$2,292	$292,456	$449,080	$700,694	$700,694		
1980	$4,535	$444,449	$444,449				
Goal			$256,000		$512,000		$1,000,000

I then ran another set of data based on the more conservative S+P 500 index fund with the following results.

Start Year	Inflation Adj. 16K in 2020	10 years Nominal	10 years 2020	20 years Nominal	20 years 2020	30 years Nominal	30 years 2020
1930	$1,066	$1,025	$18,940	$2,600	$27,973	$13,911	$122,192
1940	$866	$2,123	$22,841	$11,359	$99,775	$23,974	$167,326
1950	$1,487	$8,111	$71,246	$17,120	$119,489	$34,671	$122,335
1960	$1,822	$3,576	$24,959	$7,243	$25,557	$32,074	$66,195
1970	$2,292	$4,297	$15,162	$19,027	$39,268	$103,206	$158,478
1980	$4,535	$21,308	$43,976	$115,579	$177,477	$106,642	$127,084
1990	$7,752	$39,226	$60,233	$36,193	$43,131	$133,841	$133,841
2000	$10,420	$9,131	$10,881	$33,767	$33,767		
2010	$13,426	$47,863	$47,863				
Goal			$32,000		$64,000		$128,000

Start Year	Inflation Adj. 16K in 2020	40 years Nominal	40 years 2020	50 years Nominal	50 years 2020	60 years Nominal	60 years 2020
1930	$1,066	$29,360	$204,918	$59,460	$209,802	$263,306	$543,415
1940	$866	$48,552	$171,313	$215,001	$443,723	$1,166,220	$1,790,784
1950	$1,487	$153,535	$316,868	$832,810	$1,278,817	$768,416	$915,713
1960	$1,822	$173,978	$267,151	$160,526	$191,297	$593,624	$593,624
1970	$2,292	$95,226	$113,480	$352,145	$352,145		
1980	$4,535	$394,363	$394,363				
Goal			$256,000		$512,000		$1,000,000

Although the S+P 500 did not perform nearly as well as the IFA 100 fund, it still gave astonishing returns. For the price of a 5 year old Honda Civic you can still cover a significant chunk, if not the entirety of retirement for your child or grandchild 60 years out. If $16,000 is too much, remember that any amount is better than none. $1,000 is still a great head start, especially if paired with additional monthly contributions.

In virtually every time period in modern U.S. history the concept of the early inheritance works wonders. These historical data points certainly give validation to the concept of gifting an inheritance at birth. Most likely your index funds which should include more international stocks and small cap stocks, will perform better than the S+P 500.

With such a large timeline it would be appropriate to invest up to a quarter of the lump sum in individual stocks. Could you imagine picking up Berkshire Hathaway in 1970, Walmart in 1980, Microsoft in 1990, Amazon in 2000, or Netflix in 2010?

What If I Need To Give Less?
That's completely OK. Any amount of money is better than none. $1,000 is still way better than nothing. Alternatively giving a set amount each month into their investment account would be a fantastic solution. With 8% returns and a steady monthly contribution for 18 years of $135 a month will get to $64,000 at 18. Even getting to $16,000 is a major advantage to your grandchild and a monthly contribution of $33 a month will get them there. For $1 a day, you can start your grandchild with

substantial assets at adulthood.

What If I Want To Give More?
If you really wanted to front load giving to your grandchildren, you could give $15,000 and your spouse could give $15,000 for $30,000 total to the child, which would pretty much double the results above. You can do this every year without running into any personal tax issues, although the more you give and the more gains they have over time the longer it will take them to realize their gains and switch the investments into new tax sheltered accounts, which isn't a bad problem to have. You can always give more than $15,000 per year, but that excess will count against your lifetime estate tax and you will have to fill out a tax form for it.

Great Grandchildren:
I think it makes the most sense to assign great grandchildren as Roth IRA beneficiaries. This is the money that you will have left over at the end of your life. Most likely your children and grandchildren will all be established adults. Not only will they be established, but they will be in great financial positions and able and willing to provide financial assistance to these children. I don't think it is necessary to provide giving this far down the tree, and I think the money will be less appreciated coming from such a distant source.

If you choose to keep giving to one more generation I would split it up evenly per family branch to ensure we cover children not yet born. If your children are done having kids and you have a known number of grandchildren split the amount per branch evenly. Then divide out by the number of children. For example, with 4 grandchildren each branch would receive 25%. Then assuming it would be unlikely anyone would have more than 5 kids, assign each great grandchild a 5% share and the remainder to their parents. This way the parents have that amount of money in reserve for any future children they may have.

But wouldn't 5% be an extremely little amount of money? Well maybe not. If you follow all of these steps and hit $1 million at age 60, following the rule of 72 your money should double about every 10 years maybe even sooner depending on how aggressively you invest. If it doubles every 10 years that's $2 million at 70, $4 million at 80, and $8 million at 90. 5% of $8 million is $400,000! This is a massive amount of money. With this being gifted to a great grandchild who may be 1 year old, will make him extraordinarily wealthy during his lifetime.

Get Each Generation Involved:
Ensure your children know that there are strings to this. We are building generational wealth for them to be able to do anything, not so they can do nothing. They are expected to take similar actions for their children and grand children. They are expected to add to building generational wealth, rather than just living off of it.

CHAPTER 18: PUTTING IT TOGETHER IN A PLAN

The uncertainty so many of us feel today, many families have felt for a lifetime - if not generations - Habitat CEO Jonathon Reckford

It's not the amount that matters. What creates and secures generational wealth is the structure and nature of the assets. We want to build a framework where each generation is saving for the next two, instead of for itself. Once again this allows for compounding to have a much longer time line and for more exponential growth. This also keeps the giving close so that the people receiving the money are more appreciative of it. Another factor that needs consideration is total taxation of wealth, not just over your lifetime, but over the lifetimes of several generations.

Generation 1: You
You are the one breaking the cycle, so you will do more

heavy lifting than each subsequent generation. You are in control and you are driving this process. Your goals should be the following:

1. Getting Yourself financially independent and able to retire with dignity.
2. Give your children a deep understanding of personal finance.
3. Assist your children, generation 2, with getting to $64,000 invested as quickly as possible.
4. Assist your children with keeping costs low and cash flowing secondary education.
5. Assist your children with a down payment on their first home.
6. Give a lump sum cash investment to grandchildren, generation 3, at birth.

Generation 2: Your Children

Your children having received help from you for starting their nest eggs, getting through secondary education, and their first time home purchase will be in an excellent position to help their children, especially since you already contributed a large lump sum to them at birth. Their responsibilities and goals should include:

1. Give their children, generation 3, a deep understanding of personal finance.
2. Assist their children in cash flowing secondary education.
3. Assist their children in a first time home purchase.
4. Give a lump sum cash investment to grandchildren, generation 4, at birth.

This cycle then should continue. All of the giving is done through the parents and grandparents, with the possible exception of retirement account beneficiary status from great grandparents. The net cost for each generation is not only smaller than what it will be for you, it is also much smaller for them to set up the next generation for success than it is to directly fund their own retirement, education, and housing, due to the savings of compounding interest.

What This System Lacks:

The one glaring problem with this system is that it hands over roughly $64,000 (or more) to an 18 year old. This can certainly be dangerous. If there is a problem with responsibility level this could be a bad thing. The only way to avoid this potential error would be to put the money in a trust fund administered by the parents, but that adds a lot of complexity. *The best solution is to spend a lot of time and energy on raising responsible kids.*

Generation A: Your parents and grandparents:
Let your parents and grandparents know what you are doing. Maybe they can assist with some of your goals.
Show them what you are investing. They need to see that you are working this plan regardless and have skin in the game. They also need to know that this isn't all or nothing, any help is better than no help. I would have zero expectations of them contributing to this process. It isn't their responsibility to do so, so any money or knowledge they would be willing to add to this process would be an amazing gift. Remember YOU are the one changing your family tree.

The only stipulation I would put on gifts from older generations would be that they must be even. I would rather none of my children receive a gift if one or more would be excluded. I have a blended family and only 1 of the 4 kids I am raising is my biological child. In my situation my parents and grandparents have always treated the kids equally, so I don't have much of a worry about this, but this is an issue that could come up in other families.

- It doesn't have to be now. Planning to give a gift at a future date is a great idea. Perhaps they want to wait until they claim Social Security, are a certain age, or don't feel comfortable giving a gift prior to their death.
- Automatic small monthly contributions to their grandchildren's stockpile accounts. This could be any amount, every $1 helps!
- Contributions to college savings accounts or direct college expenses as they incur.
- Help with the lump sum contribution for their great grandchildren's accounts.
- Changing beneficiaries to grandchildren or great grandchildren from children on financial accounts.

CHAPTER 19: GOING BIG

"How do you inspire a grandchild to go to work if they know they'll never have a poor day in their life?" - Sam Walton

A few tens of thousands of dollars properly applied can absolutely change your family tree. The focus of this book is to help people with little to no assets give their children and grandchildren a leg up in life. But what if you want to really change your tree? Instead of going from poverty to upper middle class you want to launch your family into the top 1%?

Honestly to go big you just do MORE of the same thing.

Rather than paying the down payment, buy your children a house. Every year each person can give up to $15,000 to any person with no tax consequences. You and your spouse could give each child 15,000.

If your children are married, that's $30,000 to both your child and his or her spouse. If they have 2 kids that's $60,000 between the 4 of them per year that both you and your spouse can give.

You can legally give more, but then you have to fill out

a form and the contribution over $15,000 per individual gets added into your lifetime estate tax exemption. Still it is better to give away assets before they appreciate, so it may make sense for some high net worth, high income individuals to exceed the $15,000 per person gifts.

You have to fill out a gift tax form for the amount over $15,000 given to any 1 individual in a year and that amount will count against your lifetime exemption. Unless you've already hit the gift tax maximum you won't have to pay any tax, this form just starts the tally against that maximum.

For a wealthy family this may make a ton of sense. With the current lifetime exemption being $11.58 million, to avoid paying any tax in the future it may make sense to give away assets before they appreciate. As an example, let's say Grandpa Bob is single, 55 years old and has around $5 million in assets. Every 10 years his assets should double. at 65 he will have $10 million, at 75 he will have $20 million, and at 85 he will have $40 million. The vast majority of this will end up with the IRS!

Grandpa Bob lives simply and rather than waiting decides he wants to give away his inheritance now. He wants to give away $3 million across 10 grandchildren, so $300,000 each. This will leave him with $2 million. He can transfer all of this money with no taxes due. All he has to do is fill out IRS Form 709. By giving away $3 million now, he potentially avoided this $3 million growing to $24 million. He used up $2,850,000 of his lifetime exclusion, so in the future can only give away another $8.73 million.

Avoiding Inheritance Tax: 99.9% of us will avoid the inheritance tax based on size alone. The rules though could change at any time. This is another reason why end of life giving is the worst option. The aspect of lowering your estate before you die is extremely important. Right now the estate tax kicks in at $11.58 million per person, so $23.16 million for a couple. Less than 1% of people currently have enough assets to worry about this, but it very easily could be you. For people who are actively trying to build their net worth and are buying apartment buildings the odds are higher that they will reach this threshold.

The Estate tax accelerates very quickly to 40% of assets. If you and your wife have $100 million at death, the estate tax could cost you over $30 million! This is on money that you were already taxed on when you earned it! The estate tax also could change at any time by the whims of congress. In the last 20 years the estate tax has varied from being completely non existent in 2010 and the current level of an $11.58 million exemption followed by a 40% rate, to a high of only a $625,000 exemption and a 55% top rate. The estate tax laws will change substantially over the next 50 years, so transfer assets while you can!

CHAPTER 20: WHAT NOT TO DO

"Make a habit of two things: to help; or at least to do no harm." - Hippocrates

Do Not Do Nothing:

Trying matters more than anything. You become what you think about. If you think about building generational wealth and want to build wealth for yourself and your children, your thoughts will become action and it will happen. The biggest problem is that NO ONE thinks about building generational wealth. Don't wait for everything to be perfect. Take immediate imperfect action.

Do Not Put Your House In Their Names:

1. The first thing this does is gets rid of the stepped up basis advantage where when your child inherits your house their tax basis is now the current value of the home. If the house is in your child's name when you die they do not get a stepped up basis, their basis is your basis. If a house increased in value $200,000 during your ownership of it, they would owe taxes on that $200,000 when they decide to sell it.

The next problem is people often put the house in the

names of multiple children. This requires the children to agree on what to do with the house. What if one wants to sell and the other wants to live there, or what if both want to live there? This is a recipe for family discontent at best. Even worse, what if the house was put in the names of the first 3 children and after a ten year gap the parents had a fourth child and never got around to adding them onto the deed? This stuff happens. Houses need to be left in your name and specific instructions needs to be included in the will as to what is to happen to them. Wills also need to be reviewed every year to ensure accuracy.

Do Not Buy Whole Life Insurance For Your Children:

I'm appalled at how whole life plans are hocked for kids, especially the "Gerber grow up plan". For starters kids don't need life insurance because no one depends on their income. These plans also are a big ripoff. There is no return. Taking that same money and investing in a UGMA (Uniform Gift To Minors) account with a total stock market index fund would be a much better option. Buying term life insurance for your children when they become adults is an excellent, inexpensive gift.

Do Not Enable Poor Decisions:

If Jr. thinks he's going to become a youtuber paid $200,000 a year, or a pop star making millions, he needs a reality check. If his goals are to smoke weed and play nintendo, the option to stay at home and save money goes away, because he isn't trying. This goes back to constantly reinforcing the values of hard work, thrift, and having a strong moral compass into your children.

> *Every man leaves a legacy behind. The quality or inferiority of your legacy will be determined by your decisions and your habits. We must em-*

ploy sustainable means of building generational wealth, but a proper legacy goes beyond just generational wealth in a form of available cash and assets. We need to pass down the knowledge of how we built the wealth, how to expend it, and how to sustain it. It is utter foolishness that we built wealth, while at the same time, allow those who are supposed to succeed us and inherit from us have a habit of consuming wealth in an unsustainable manner. We must teach our kids to Think! Cause a fool and his money are soon parted. - Ntshuxeko Ndlovu

Do Not Buy Them New Cars:

The most frequent action I see parents doing to "help" their children is buying them new cars when they turn 16 or graduate high school. This is a really unwise move. Cars are a depreciating asset. Every day that car becomes worth less in value. Most of these parents aren't paying cash, so these cars have loans on them that the parents are paying. That debt service is hindering the parent from building wealth. Cars with loans on them require full coverage insurance. Full coverage insurance for a teenage driver is through the roof.

The really big issue is that it makes the children accustomed to driving a nice vehicle. They will see driving a new vehicle as normal and will always be broke. They will be paying a large chunk of their income towards interest, depreciation, and insurance, all the while having a large amount of their net worth tied up in a vehicle. After 5 or 6 years they then restart with a new car and will always have a car payment.

Don't buy them a new car. Help them buy a decent used car in the $1,000 to $5,000 range.

Do Not Use Dynasty Trusts:

Dynasty trusts are trusts designed to last for several hundred years. Each state has different laws for how long trusts can last for. Many states over the past 50 years have greatly expanded this time line. Dynasty trusts are an estate planning tool typically used by the ultra rich, the top 0.1%. The main goal of a dynasty trust is to avoid estate tax being assessed to multiple generations.

With a dynasty trust when the founder of the trust funds it, depending on the size, estate taxes may be owed, but after that every subsequent generation is shielded from the inheritance tax because the trust is the owner of the assets and the beneficiaries only receive income generated by the trust.

The grantor of the trust can set up stipulations under what circumstances beneficiaries can receive money from the trust. These are highly complicated, expensive legal structures that are not necessary or ideal for the vast majority of people. If an estate planning lawyer is trying to sell you on this, they are likely looking out for their own best interest over yours, as they would earn yearly administration fees from the trust.

Taxes and changes in tax law are also a major caution with dynasty trusts. Believe it or not, the tax laws in the United States change fairly often and from time to time there is a lot of anti-wealth sentiment in this country. I would not be surprised if in the futures vehicles such as dynasty trusts are given extremely high tax rates, if not outright seized. For all of these reasons I don't think that dynasty trusts are the best way to go about building generational wealth, at leat for 99.9% of us.

CHAPTER 21: ASSISTING OTHERS ON THEIR JOURNEY

May I never get too busy in my own affairs that I fail to respond to the needs of others with kindness and compassion - Thomas Jefferson

Once you have a framework in place to get your kids on the right path help others as well. Whether this is nieces and nephews, friends, or complete strangers. Gifting transformational assets is a highly desireable option.

Debt Reduction:

My favorite charity is RIP Medical Debt, and over the years I have contributed thousands of dollars towards this charity. RIP Medical Debt buys up old medical debt in bulk and because of the bulk purchases buys it for one cent or less on the dollar. RIP Medical Debt then forgives this debt which leaves no tax consequences for the recipients. So far they have forgiven over $4 billion in medical debt. I love that the leverage is 1:100. For every $100 of donations you pay off $10,000 in medical debt. RIP Medical Debt also is eligible for many corporate matching programs so this leverage can often be 1:200 meaning a $100 donation can pay off $20,000 in medical debt!

Education Programs:

The Dolly Parton Imagination Library is another great program to support. The imagination library sends 1 book per month to kids from birth to age 5. These age appropriate books encourage a love for reading and bridge the literacy gap between middle class children and children in poverty. Over 1.7 million children have been registered with over 150 million books given away. The program is supported by different non profits in each geographic area. In my area the local United Way facilitates the program. Most of these local facilitators as well as the overall program are eligible for corporate matching programs as well.

The Mike Rowe Works Scholarship is my favorite scholarship fund. This scholarship program is designed to help young people entering the skilled trades reach their goals. Each year roughly 200 scholarships of varying amounts are issued.

> "The Work Ethic Scholarship Program is about recognizing the people who understand the importance of personal responsibility, delayed gratification, a positive attitude, and, of course, work ethic. The hardworking men and women who keep the lights on, water running, and air flowing—the next generation of skilled workers who will work smart and hard. These are the folks we consider rock stars, and we want to reward them." - Mike Rowe Works

Financial Guidance:

If you have limited funds, gifting financial guidance to someone who is willing to receive it can change their life. Start out with a few select books from Appendix I. Be a mentor and check in with them on a monthly basis to help them stay on track.

Baby Shower UGMA Gifts:

Doing this in the same light as the lump sum contributions to your grandchildren's accounts at birth. A $1,000 lump sum at birth is still a major benefit to any child. The existence of the account will also make it easier for the parents/grandparents to add to it as time goes on.

Business Launch Shower:

If someone in your circle is starting a small business, host a shower for them, just like a baby shower! Invite people to come together to help buy supplies and equipment to give them a lift off the ground and contribute what you can both monetarily and with guidance.

Gifting An Emergency Fund:

For most people an emergency fund is a life changer. The vast majority of Americans live paycheck to paycheck. Gifting an emergency fund of a few thousand dollars can literally change someone's life. This could completely eliminate the scarcity mindset. Sure someone could squander it on a big screen TV and Playstation 5, but odds are for someone truly struggling that is receptive to help, they may end up surprising you. No matter what they do with the money, once you give it it is theirs. Don't gift it with the expectation that it must be used only as an emergency fund. You can suggest it, but once you write the check it is their money. Don't cause yourself heartache because someone else didn't use a gift exactly as you would have.

Monthly UGMA Contributions To Children:

While contributing to your children's Stockpile accounts, offer to open one for your friend's child and gift a steady automatic deposit. This could be as little as $10 a month and still make a big difference over the long term.

Down Payment Assistance:

This is the big one. The largest barrier to home ownership is a down payment. Consider helping a motivated friend or family member with a down payment gift or a matching fund down payment gift.

CHAPTER 22: ECONOMIC POLICY TO INCREASE THE MEDIAN WEALTH

"I am arguing nothing less than asset based public policy. In conjunction with living wages and adequate social assistance policies that motivate families to accumulate assets for education, home ownership, business development, retirement, and emergencies can best launch family mobility, well being, and self reliance...The distinction between income based survival policies and asset based mobility strategies clearly isolates the main shortcomings of contemporary welfare reform policies, which confuse welfare caseload reduction with lifting families out of poverty." - Thomas M. Shapiro The Hidden Cost of Being African American

It's not lost on me that this is a difficult road for any family. Difficult, but not impossible. The number one rule of economics is that people respond to incentives and the incentives that we have structurally do not support the building of wealth for the masses of society. I propose that our country make the following changes to promote the building of generational wealth in our society.

Personal Finance Education In Schools:

The personal finance education in schools is the starting point. Our kids graduate high school without knowing how to start a business, how to file taxes, and of course without knowing how to build wealth or how compounding interest works. I'm advocating for 250 hours of personal finance education spread from 6th grade through senior year.

We need to have a class that teaches people how to start a business. We need to have a class that teaches people how to file their taxes and what tax credits and other tax breaks exist.

We need a class that teaches people how to buy a house. Everything from knowing when you can afford to buy a house to how to get financing, and what different closing costs are. A loan amortization schedule should be readily identifiable.

And of course we need to teach our children about compounding interest while they are in school. This shouldn't be some dry finance class. This is exciting stuff, especially with how much time they have for investments to grow.

We do a great disservice to our children and to society

as a whole by leaving them completely financially uneducated. This needs to change and it needs to change now. If we are going to have the Federal government involved in education it absolutely needs to be teaching these basics across the board, whether the kids are in a rich school or poor school, in Alaska or Florida.

Baby Stocks: $5,000 At Birth:

This proposal to government assistance will perhaps make the largest dent in the wealth gap. This proposal is similar to the "Baby Bonds" proposal introduced by Senator Corey Booker, but using the stock market for higher returns. Compounding interest is the best way to build long term wealth and the easiest intervention is at birth, because this gives the most time for the money to grow. 18 years is a long enough window that a total stock market index fund makes a lot more sense than bonds. We have about 3.8 million births per year in this country. 3.8 million births X $1,000 is 3.8 billion. X 5 is $19 Billion per year. pocket change for our country. If we can spend close to $4 trillion a year, we can find $20 billion on investing in our citizens early on. This early intervention is the most bang for your tax dollars we can get.

As a way to reduce costs we could even have an adjustment here where a phaseout begins for families at 300% of FPL (Federal Poverty Level) and drops it to a floor of 25% of the total credit for families at 500% of FPL or above. This could cut the total yearly cost to under $15 billion.

Corey Booker's plan, which is a bit more complicated and has yearly contributions based on family income shows that by JUST doing this would increase the median wealth among young Black Americans from $2,900 to $57,845, and for young White Americans from $46,000 to $79,159. Instead of White Americans having 16 times the wealth of Black Americans, this would drop to under 1.5 times.

This $19 Billion a year plan is 1/3 the cost of Corey Booker's plan, but the median result is about the same due to funding more money earlier and to stock market returns of 8% over government bond returns of 3% or less. Don't get me wrong, I am not opposed to Corey Booker's plan, I just think this is a better overall solution. Alternatively it could follow his plan 100%, with the parent being able to choose between an all bond, an all stock, and a "target retirement date" mixed fund. ANY steps towards some sort of gift at birth for children of this country is a step in the right direction.

$5,000 invested at 8% will be $21,000 at 18. This money would NOT count as assets against any means tested programs. Starting out with roughly $21,000 will give every child a major leg up in launching in life. This is an emergency fund, education expenses, retirement savings, or business and investing seed money.

As a rider to this I would like to see the 1040 tax form have a spot to automatically send a portion of your refund into your children's compounding interest accounts. You could select to have 10%, 20%, or 50% of your refund deposited into their accounts with a checkbox. This money would be evenly spread into the accounts of all the children claimed on the tax return.

Retirement Incentives:

We do incentives for saving for retirement backwards. I strongly believe that this change will be a big factor in getting a much larger portion of our society ready for retirement. We highly reward people with high incomes for saving for retirement, while giving sometimes zero incentive for people with low incomes to save for retirement. If you are in the 0% tax bracket a tax deduction does you no good, and saving any for retirement is a really hard thing to do.

If you are in the 35% tax bracket saving for retirement is comparatively easy because you have a lot of disposable income, you get a 35% assistance from the federal government, AND you're more likely to have employer matching. A dual earning household earning $450,000 a year and maxing their 401Ks at $39,000 per year will receive over $13,000 in retirement incentives per year from the federal government. These high earners are also more likely to already have an incentive to save for retirement in the form of an employer match. In this income bracket a 5% match would gain them another $22,500 in additional retirement savings. Retirement contributions are also deductible from state income taxes. Using California's 9.3% income tax bracket this couple would get an additional $3,627 in state tax incentives. By saving $39,000 they received an additional $39,777 in total immediate incentives, more than their total contributions!

By contrast, a single mom earning $30,000 a year and saving $3,000 will receive no tax benefit from saving for retirement and is less likely to receive a 401K match from an employer.

Retirement Incentives By Income Level		
Income	$450,000	$30,000
Retirement Savings	$39,000	$3,000
Employer Match	$22,500	$0
Federal Tax Break	$13,650	$0
CA State Tax Break	$3,627	$0
Total Incentives	$39,777	$0
Incentives as % of Savings	101.99%	0.00%

What about the existing retirement savers tax credit? The idea is good, but since it is not refundable there is no incentive for low earners with kids to save for retirement. With the doubling of the child tax credit this has become an unusable vestige of the old tax code.

What we need to do is have a refundable retirement savers tax credit with incentives up to $5,000 instead of $2,000 and pay for it by reducing the tax deduction on 401K plans. I envision making the 401K tax deduction freeze at 20% for those in higher tax brackets. This flattening of the bracket will lower the benefit received by top earners, while still keeping a strong incentive to save in place. Low income earners would then be able to use a refundable retirement savers tax credit that is between 20% to 50% of the value of their retirement savings based on income, with a maximum benefit based off of $5,000 in contributions, so a maximum of $2,500 of benefit per year.

Psychologically a low earner weighing the trade off of investing in a retirement account vs. not investing is seeing instead of $1 going into an account he or she can't touch for decades, that $1 can go to an immediate need.

> "When resources are low or scarce, the rational decision is to take the immediate benefit and to discount future gain" -Mellisa Sturge Apple: The Color of Money.

A high earner who has all his or her immediate needs covered anyways will psychologically see not investing in a retirement account as throwing away between 35 cents and $1.48 (depending on the employer match and state tax rate). In the higher tax bracket its absolutely crazy to not max your retirement accounts, its an automatic minimum of a 35% return right off the bat. For a low earner it's a break even game with where to allocate money, and with no incentives very few actually go with putting it away for the long term. Our incentives make savings for retirement a no brainer for high earners (who likely have more education and more assets than low earners) and a really difficult decision for lower earners.

For a high earner there is an instant gratification of both the employer match and the tax deduction as well as the long term reward of tax free compounding. For low earners there is no instant gratification, only the long term reward of tax free compounding. Since we are wired to think for short term, instant gratification, we are tipping the scales in an even greater direction to the high earners than what the tax code already is doing.

This vast difference in incentives also explains the vast

difference between studies showing average retirement savings and median retirement savings. The top 10% of income earners are saving a ton of money, while the bottom 50% are barely saving any.

Home Ownership:

We should have a national down payment assistance program. Most often the largest barrier to home ownership is the down payment. Down payment assistance programs already exist in many states, but should be standardized across the country. These should be up to 3.5% to cover the minimum FHA down payment of the home, provided they otherwise qualify for the loan and go through a first time home buyer class to ensure first time home buyers learn how to protect themselves when buying a home. My state has a program similar to this, but it is poorly promoted. Every bank should be advertising these programs. These classes should also include in them negotiating for the seller to pay for some of their closing costs, further reducing total cash out of pocket to buy a home. This program could be jointly funded between state governments and the Federal government.

We should also open up sub $50K loans. Another problem is that many lenders won't issue home loans under $50,000. This magnifies the wealth gap further because in many poor Black neighborhoods the median house costs under $50,000. Instead of needing to come up with a 3.5% down payment, or even a 20% down payment, the barrier to buying a home becomes a 100% cash purchase.

Since the federal government underwrites most mortgages through the FHA/Freddie Mac/Fannie Mae programs, there is room here to encourage lending on low dollar homes. I think the easiest method to encourage banks to lend on these properties is to add a $1,000 bounty for closing owner occupied loans to qualified applicants for homes under $50,000. The banks would earn an extra $1,000 and credit would flow. This is a relatively low cost social engineering method that will bring way more than its cost back into the value of the community. This small incentive, even if 1 million people become home owners from it per year it would still only cost $1 billion in total funding.

The risky subprime loans that were issued leading to the great recession did not have much in the way of a safety valve built in. In order to reduce risk on the subprime loans I am advocating that the loans could only be issued for 15 year mortgages. In the event of another mortgage crisis the banks would have a profitable option of loan modification to a 30 year loan which would give the bank more interest income and lower the monthly payments for the home owner. With today's interest rates a 15 year loan 5 years in will be 30% paid off, compared to a 30 year loan which would only be 11% paid off.

CHAPTER 23: ECONOMIC POSSIBILITIES FOR OUR GRANDCHILDREN

"The difficulty lies not so much in developing new ideas as in escaping from old ones." - John Maynard Keynes

In 1930 economist John Maynard Keynes published the essay "Economic Possibilities For Our Grandchildren". This essay postulates on what the nature of work and life could be in 100 years. As of the writing of this book we are only 9 years away from his predicted time frame. Below are excerpts from this essay. I highly recommend reading the entire essay as well.

> *"My purpose in this essay, however, is not to examine the present or the near future, but to disembarrass myself of short views and take wings into*

the future. What can we reasonably expect the level of our economic life to be a hundred years hence? What are the economic possibilities for our grandchildren?

What is the result? In spite of an enormous growth in the population of the world, which it has been necessary to equip with houses and machines, the average standard of life in Europe and the United States has been raised, I think, about fourfold. The growth of capital has been on a scale which is far beyond a hundredfold of what any previous age had known. And from now on we need not expect so great an increase of population....

But this is only a temporary phase of maladjustment. All this means in the long run that mankind is solving its economic problem. I would predict that the standard of life in progressive countries one hundred years hence will be between four and eight times as high as it is to-day. There would be nothing surprising in this even in the light of our present knowledge. It would not be foolish to contemplate the possibility of a far greater progress still.

Let us, for the sake of argument, suppose that a hundred years hence we are all of us, on the average, eight times better off in the economic sense than we are to-day. Assuredly there need be nothing here to surprise us...

Now it is true that the needs of human beings may seem to be insatiable. But they fall into two classes --those needs which are absolute in the sense that we feel them whatever the situation of our fellow human beings may be, and those which are relative in the sense that we feel them only if their satisfaction lifts us above, makes us feel superior to, our fellows. Needs of the second class, those which satisfy the desire for superiority, may indeed be insatiable; for the higher the general level, the higher still are they. But this is not so true of the absolute needs-a point may soon be reached, much sooner perhaps than we are all of us aware of, when these needs are satisfied in the sense that we prefer to devote our further energies to non-economic purposes...

Absolute needs being food, water, shelter, heat, and clothing. Relative "needs" are a $400,000 house vs. a $40,000 house, a $40,000 car versus a $1,000 car, 70" TVs, eating out every night, and designer clothes.

Now for my conclusion, which you will find, I think, to become more and more startling to the imagination the longer you think about it. I draw the conclusion that, assuming no important wars and no important increase in population, the economic problem may be solved, or be at least within sight of solution, within a hundred years. This means that the economic problem is not-if we look into the future-the permanent problem of the human race.

Why, you may ask, is this so startling? It is startling because-if, instead of looking into the future, we look into the past-we find that the economic problem, the struggle for subsistence, always has been hitherto the primary, most pressing problem of the human race-not only of the human race, but of the whole of the biological kingdom from the beginnings of life in its most primitive forms.

Thus we have been expressly evolved by nature-with all our impulses and deepest instincts-for the purpose of solving the economic problem. If the economic problem is solved, mankind will be deprived of its traditional purpose.

Thus for the first time since his creation man will be faced with his real, his permanent problem-how to use his freedom from pressing economic cares, how to occupy the leisure, which science and compound interest will have won for him, to live wisely and agreeably and well.

The strenuous purposeful money-makers may carry all of us along with them into the lap of economic abundance. But it will be those peoples, who can keep alive, and cultivate into a fuller perfection, the art of life itself and do not sell themselves for the means of life, who will be able to enjoy the abundance when it comes.

Technological advances AND compounding interest are necessary for the standards of living to improve. Those who don't invest can't benefit from compounding interest. Invest early! Technological advances have rendered food cheaper and more plentiful, access to the worlds knowledge via the internet and instant communication with anyone in the world is virtually free. This allows people to work many more jobs remotely from anywhere in the world, allowing us to choose to live in low cost of living areas.

Yet there is no country and no people, I think, who can look forward to the age of leisure and of abundance without a dread. For we have been trained too long to strive and not to enjoy. It is a fearful problem for the ordinary person, with no special talents, to occupy himself, especially if he no longer has roots in the soil or in custom or in the beloved conventions of a traditional society.

For many ages to come the old Adam will be so strong in us that everybody will need to do some work if he is to be contented. We shall do more things for ourselves than is usual with the rich today, only too glad to have small duties and tasks and routines. But beyond this, we shall endeavour

> to spread the bread thin on the butter-to make what work there is still to be done to be as widely shared as possible. Three-hour shifts or a fifteen-hour week may put off the problem for a great while. For three hours a day is quite enough to satisfy the old Adam in most of us!

> Of course there will still be many people with intense, unsatisfied purposiveness who will blindly pursue wealth-unless they can find some plausible substitute. But the rest of us will no longer be under any obligation to applaud and encourage them.

I find myself being drawn to this. I can live comfortably for the rest of my life on a net worth of $600,000, but when I run the numbers and see that if I work two more decades I could amass a total net worth of over $100,000,000 in my lifetime I'm drawn to keep working to invest more.

> I look forward, therefore, in days not so very remote, to the greatest change which has ever occurred in the material environment of life for human beings in the aggregate. But, of course, it will all happen gradually, not as a catastrophe. Indeed, it has already begun. The course of affairs will simply be that there will be ever larger and larger classes and groups of people from whom problems of economic necessity have been practically removed. The critical difference will be realised when this condition has become so general

> \that the nature of one's duty to one's neighbour is changed. For it will remain reasonable to be economically purposive for others after it has ceased to be reasonable for oneself.

This is the important part. It doesn't happen all at once. It is a gradual change and more and more people are going to "get it"; first the high earners, then normal retirees, then the FIRE (Financial Indepence Retire Early) crowd, then their kids, then the masses will start as well. The concept of the masses retiring in their 60's was not the norm in 1930.

> The pace at which we can reach our destination of economic bliss will be governed by four things-our power to control population, our determination to avoid wars and civil dissensions, our willingness to entrust to science the direction of those matters which are properly the concern of science, and the rate of accumulation as fixed by the margin between our production and our consumption; of which the last will easily look after itself, given the first three."

Controlling population growth is pretty much solved. Population growth in the US and most of the world has flat-lined, with average births per woman below 2.0. We have of course had several wars since this was written, and the size and scope of the United State Government has greatly increased. The final point on us needing to produce more than we consume to accrue capital is where on the individual level and on the Federal Government level we are failing, which is delaying widespread reductions in working hours and increases in wealth accumulation.

We still average the same working hours as someone did in 1940, despite a century long downward trend in work hours from a peak of 70 hours per week to the trough of around 40 hours per week in 1940. We are no where near a 15 hour standard work week. If you read the quote above he talks about some "needs" of man to be insatiable. The needs for competition and to feel superior to his common man. Ever hear of keeping up with the Jones's? This is what he was talking about. The primary reason we are working more is that we as individuals are constantly buying "stuff" and live well beyond our means, never allowing capital for ourselves to accumulate. A good example is the overall US increase in spending on housing and the size of our houses. In 1930 the average new house was just under 1,000 square feet, today it is 2,400.

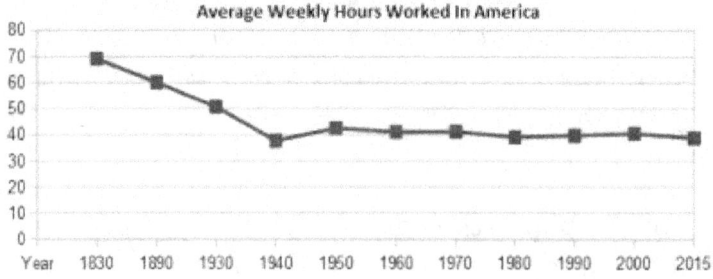

As our income increases we are more likely to move up in house and cars. It's not uncommon for people with a 6 figure income to buy $500,000 houses in an area where the median house is $150,000 and to have 2 luxury cars in the driveway. This is exacerbated by financial planners presenting the rule of thumb that we need 80% of our pre-retirement income to retire. This means that as we make more money we need to have an ever larger nest egg. With a moving goal post we get trapped and never reduce work hours.

If you chose to live a normal standard of living in 1930 then this could absolutely be done on a 15 hour work week. The average person lived in a rural area in a house that was put together with scrap materials. There were no building codes, and much of the nation didn't have electricity or natural gas. There were 26 million registered cars in 1930 when we had a population of 123 million people. Today there are 273 million cars for a population of 328 million people.

By taking advantage of the scales of industry that have reduced the cost of our most basic needs, such as food, utilities, shelter, and transportation, we absolutely can live a comfortable life on 15 hours of work per week.

CHAPTER 24: POSSIBILITIES FOR A 15 HOUR WORK WEEK

"People who live far below their means enjoy a freedom that people busy upgrading their lifestyle can't fathom" - Naval Ravikant

15 Hour Work Week Option 1: Live Cheaply:

I know that most people reading the last section probably found the idea of a 15 hour work week laughable. Most Americans are struggling on a 40 hour work week. It is possible to live a lot cheaper than our current societal norms. Try to achieve a standard of living equal to that of people in 1930. This isn't easy at all, but it is possible.

Live in a low cost of living area. Benton Harbor, MI is a perfect example. You can buy a decent livable house for $40,000. (I've bought 5 houses in Benton Harbor for less than this amount.) With a 5%, $2,000 down payment and a $38,000 15 year mortgage at 2.5% there would be a payment of $253 a month. Insurance is $31 per month and taxes on this house would be $54 per month for total housing costs of **$338** per month.

Let's add in another **$150** per month to save towards capital expenditures, things like future roof replacements and furnace replacements.

Utilities: Many of the houses in this area are on a well and septic system, meaning no water and sewer bill. Electric and gas combined should average to under **$150** per month.

Vehicles: A $1,000 vehicle has the same utility as a $40,000 vehicle. I've averaged 5 years out of each $1,000 vehicle I've driven. Driving a $1,000 vehicle means no car payments and very little depreciation. A $1,000 vehicle that lasts 5 years and gets scrapped for $200 then costs $13.33 per month. Double this to cover maintenance and repairs and you get **$26 per month** for a vehicle. Add in $100 for fuel/oil changes and $50 for insurance and we have **$176 total per month**. A car is also not a necessity and biking could be a primary transportation method, costing literally nothing per month.

Groceries: Buy food in bulk and cook from scratch. Oatmeal for breakfast, rice and vegetable for lunch, and a small chunk of pork, fish, or chicken with rice and vegetables for dinner. Drink water rather than beer, pop, and fruit juices. Most of what we spend on food is optional. Eating out is optional. Pop tarts, Doritos, and microwave pizzas are optional. A diet such as this per person can cost as little as $2 a day.

- Rice 25# bag $15
- 50# sack of potatoes: $20
- 5# carrots: $5
- 10# oats: $10
- 6# of meat at $2 per pound: (3oz serving per day) $12

Total: **$62 per month.** This is highly simplistic, but it is achievable to spend <$100 per month on groceries for 1 person.

Clothing: Each year 5 pairs of discount jeans, a 5 pack of shirts, a pack of underwear, socks, and a pair of work boots: $300 for the year, divided by 12 months is **$25 per month.** This is actually more than what I personally spend on clothing per year.

For a "low income" individual or family health care in this country is free through the Affordable Care Act marketplace. I'll add in another **$100 per month** for dental expenses which are not covered by health insurance.

So far we have housing, transportation, food, utilities, medical care, and clothing covered at a total cost of $1,001 a month. Of these items for a multi-person household food and clothing are the only ones that will increase to any substantial degree. Adding **$100 extra per person** to this budget fills in these holes. A family of 3 could live this lifestyle on $1,200 a month. Note that one parent could stay at home on such a low family budget so no child care is needed.

Taxes: On $1,200 a month in earnings no federal income or state taxes would be owed, only Social Security and Medicare taxes of 7.45%. This would require closer to

$1,300 a month in total income.

Misc: $200: We want to have a bit of breathing room in the budget, so let's arrive at a **$1,500 per month total budget.**

Work Hours to 15 per week per person: $1,500 per month is $375 per week. Because this household is made up of 2 adults and only one is working, the one working could work 30 hours per week so that as a couple they are averaging 15 hours. Working 30 hours per week would require a wage of **$12.50 per hour.** Anything over this amount and the family would have a surplus. There are plenty of jobs that pay much higher than this rate.

(Note: I realize I did this math based on 4 weeks per month, which shorted 4 weeks out of the calendar year, therefore our main character would have an extra $1,500 per year in earnings.)

Tax Returns: This family of 3 would receive a $3,500 Earned Income Credit tax refund and a $3,000 Child Tax Refund each year. This extra $6,500 would help the family with large expenses and to use some of their income towards wealth building.

Is this budget and lifestyle ideal? Not by our standards today, but it is POSSIBLE. It's also still a much higher standard of living than what most people had in 1930, especially when you add in the time advantage. This is starting out with only $2,000 for a down payment. No family wealth, no high paying job. Just earning $12.50 an hour and never getting a raise. This family has to be focused on their budget but this is feasible. $12.50 is the minimum income to achieve this.

If he focuses on increasing his wages over time any increase in pay rate will substantially change his standard of living. There are temporary and part time jobs, as well as small businesses that can be started that can pay over twice per hour what we are using in this example.

The point is that with thoughtful planning and some sacrifices it is possible to live inexpensively and thus to live off of working 15 hours per week if we choose to trade extra stuff and lifestyle for time. Don't like this budget? Then shoot to earn $25 an hour to double it. There are plenty of jobs and small businesses where you can earn $25 an hour.

What's really great about this lifestyle is the built in check valve of being able to work more hours if needed. If your life is based on both spouses working 40+ hours a week, the ability to work more hours to earn more money if needed for a specific life event or emergency is severely hindered. If only working 30 hours total, there are far more hours available to use to increase income in such a situation.

Compound Interest:

Let's take this a step further and add in compounding interest to the equation. The US stock market for the last 100 years has returned right around 10%. There are many funds and sectors that have exceeding this by several percentage points. For the exercise of this example I will use 10% returns, which is more conservative than the 12% Dave Ramsey uses and more aggressive than the 6% financial planners that carry an umbrella with them if there is a single cloud in the sky recommend.

I've written a lot about compounding interest. The longer capital has to grow the more it compounds and the higher the amount of money is. Because we are looking at using the gains off of this nest egg at a young age to buy more time I will do all the math here with a 4% withdrawal rate. A 4% withdrawal rate is hyper conservative.

15 Hour Work Week Option 2: Build Wealth Quickly

Instead of moving out right at 18, buying a house, and starting a family, let's assume the subject of our story lived at his parents home for five years while working 40 hours per week earning $12 per hour. This would equate to $25,000 per year in earnings and since he has no expenses he invests 75% of his income. After five years between his investments and their growth he will have $120,000. It has not been the historical norm to kick kids out of the house once they hit 18 or graduate from high school. This is a relatively modern development. In 1930 it was very common for adult children to live at home for several years. We do a great disservice to our children by not having them stay at home and bank cash like crazy for a few years.

He then buys his house at 23 and follows the budget outlined above, but works 40 hours at $12.50 instead of 30 hours. This is still a major improvement over the status quo which would have both partners working 40 hours for 80 total, per person they are at 20 hours per week average. Now, he invests the extra $500 per month he is earning and half of his tax return which equates to $204 per month. He does this from 23 to 33. At 33 his investment account will have grown to $469,000. A 4% draw from this would be $1,563 per month, enough to fully replace the families expenses, AND it would still be growing in value every year.

At 33 he tapers down to 30 hours per week of work, allowing compounding interest to have bought him more time. His nest egg is just fine without him adding more to it, so just stopping retirement contributions buys him 10 hours per week. At this point he is at just over $3,000 in total income and his family can start spending much more money than the bare bones budget they had for 10 years. 5 years later the house is paid off, eliminating $253 per month of expenses.

Because he has been drawing out 4% of the remaining balance at the start of each year, the growth in his investment account has slowed to 6%.

- At 40 he has $714,000 allowing him to withdrawal $2,380 per month. With a paid off house and substantially more in his nest egg he can cut back hours again, this time to 15 total hours. This would bring in $750 per week, allowing for a total budget of $3,130 per month. Remember the house is paid off, all retirement savings is done, and there are no federal or state income taxes owed.
- At 50 he has $1,300,000 allowing him to withdrawal $4,333 per month. At this point he stops working entirely. The $4,333 is enough income to meet his families needs.
- At 60 he has $2,365,000 allowing him to withdrawal $7,883 per month

In this example our main character never got a raise, his

spouse never earned any income, and he never sold his house and moved up, pocketing a capital gain.

Career Ark:

Here's how his work hours compared to the typical family's weekly total work hours.

- 18-22: 40 hours Vs 40 hours
- 23-32: 40 hours Vs. 80 hours
- 33-39: 30 hours Vs 80 hours
- 40-49: 15 hours Vs 80 hours
- 50 - 64 0 hours Vs 80 hours

Lifetime work hours for our couple (assuming 2 weeks vacation per year): Across a 47 year working career our couple worked a total of 48,000 hours compared to the Jones' who worked 178,000 hours. The Jones' averaged 36.4 hours per week per person person year. Our couple averaged 9.8 hours per person per week across 47 years, and had $3.2 million at 65, whereas the median Jones' would have $58,000. How on Earth is this possible?

The gains from investing a lot and investing early coupled with living well below their means.

15 Hour Work Week Option 3: Generational Wealth:

I plan to give my grandchildren $16,000 at birth to put in an investment account in their names. By 18 these accounts would grow to $96,000. I encourage all financially stable grandparents to do the same. If they can't afford $16,000 then any amount, even $1,000 will make a big difference.

If their parents also contributed $10 per week from their

cash flow plus 1/2 of the child tax credit they receive, they would be adding $126 per month, which would see the account grow to **$171,000 at 18**.

Now we repeat the same first step as option 1. Our main character stays at home for five years, works 40 hours a week, and invests 75% of his income. Earning $12 per hour his investments would grow to $120,000 over 5 years. During that same time the $171,000 he already had at 18 would grow to $281,000, for a combined total of $452,000 at 23 years of age!

A 4% withdrawal rate would give him $1,500 per month, enough to cover all the expenses in the bare bones budget described earlier. Working 15 hours per week starting at 23 would allow him to bring in $750 a month, in addition to the $1,500 from his investments for a total income of $2,250 per month. Continuing to withdrawal 4% of the balance of his nest egg without investing any more money, his nest egg would grow at 6% to:

- At 30: $647,000, he can withdrawal $2,156 per month
- At 40: $1,177,000, he can withdrawal $3,923 per month. At this point working no longer makes sense. He can more than cover all his families expenses with a large buffer.
- At 50: $2,174,000, he can withdrawal $7,246 per month and easily fund large gifts at birth for his grandchildren, continuing the tradition.
- At 60: $3,898,000, he can withdrawal $12,993 per month.

In this example our main character never got a raise, his spouse never earned any income, and he never sold his house and moved up, pocketing a capital gain.

Career Ark:

- 18-22: worked 40 hours per week
- 23-39 worked 15 hours per week
- 40-64 worked 0 hours per week.

Lifetime total hours worked: 22,750. Compared to the Jones' 178,000 hours. Across 47 years this is an average of 4.7 hours per week per person compared to the Jones' 36.4. Our protagonist also has $5,258,000 in his investment account at 65, compared to the Jones' $58,000.

A 15 hour work week is not impossible. Keynes was right that the 15 hour work week would be possible for an ever growing segment of society. Ask yourself, what actions am I taking to live a more purposeful life, be more efficient with money, and ultimately reduce my working hours?

CHAPTER 25: CONCLUSION

Knowledge without action is wastefulness and action without knowledge is foolishness - Al-Ghazali

I wrote this book to inspire others to change their family trees. I strongly believe that our societal advancements and compounding interest have brought the ability for those not born into royalty or wealth the ability to at a minimum remove themselves and their heirs from poverty, as well as greatly reducing their lifetime work hours from the "normal" 47 years of 40 hours a week for two people.

This freedom will ultimately unlock the time and creative energy of our children and grandchildren to further benefit mankind, and of course improve the quality of their individual lives as well.

You can have all the knowledge in the world, but it means nothing if you don't take consistent action. I challenge you to start today to take some action, no matter how small to improve your finances today, and every day into the future.

Thank you for reading my book "*For My Children's Children*", writing this has been an extremely rewarding experience for me, and I am thankful to be able to share my ideas and what I have learned over the years with others. If you have found this book to be insightful and have gained value from it, please share this book with your family and friends by posting on Facebook and other social media.

I would greatly appreciate it if you could take the time to give an honest review of this book on Amazon.com. Your feedback will help me write future books, make revisions to this book, and help other readers decide if this is a book they would benefit from.

APPENDIX I: BOOK SUGGESTIONS

The Legacy Journey - Dave Ramsey

The Millionaire Next Door - Thomas J. Stanley

Everyday Millionaires - Chris Hogan

Thou Shall Prosper - Rabbi Daniel Lapin

163 Ways to Pursue Excellence - Tom Peters

Start with Why - Simon Senek

Rich Dad Poor Dad - Robert Kiyosaki

The Color of Money - Mehrsa Baradaran

The Kids Roth IRA Handbook - Tracy Foote

The Opposite of Spoiled - Ron Lieber

Turn $100 Into $1,000,000 - James McKinna

The Hidden Cost of Being African American - Thomas Shapiro

APPENDIX II
COMPOUND
INTEREST CHARTS

I have made several charts to demonstrate the power of compounding interest. These charts are built with a consistent annual return, however in reality the yearly annual return will be highly variable. The return I am using mathematically works out to the annualized return over the entire period of time.

The contributions are assigned at the beginning of the year. If they were contributing throughout the year like most contributions are the math would be slightly different than the numbers presented here, however this would be a statistical rounding error.

This set of master spreadsheets can be downloaded at Actionecon.com for free to experiment with, track your progress and run your own scenarios.
Fig A: Investing 3K/year from 16-65 with 12% returns.

Fig B: Investing 3K/year from 16-65 with 10% returns.

Fig C: Investing 3K/year from 16-65 with 8% returns.

Fig D: Investing 16K at birth with 8% returns.

Fig E: Investing 16K/year from 33-65 with 8% returns. Note this ends up at roughly the same value at age 64 as investing $16K as a one time contribution at birth.

Fig F: Investing 3K/year from 35-65 with 8% returns. This is more typical of what the average person does.

Fig G: Investing 50% of earnings from 16-21 while living at home and getting 8% returns.

Fig H: Investing 50% of income from 16-21 while living at home, then saving 10K/yr and getting 8% returns.

Fig I: $100/mo parent contribution 0-18 plus saving half of income from 6 to 18 getting 8% returns.

FOR MY CHILDREN'S CHILDREN

Fig A: $3,000 Per Year With 12% Gains

Age	Starting Balance	Contribution	Gain	End of Year
16	$0	$3,000	$360	$3,360
17	$3,360	$3,000	$763	$7,123
18	$7,123	$3,000	$1,215	$11,338
19	$11,338	$3,000	$1,721	$16,059
20	$16,059	$3,000	$2,287	$21,346
21	$21,346	$3,000	$2,921	$27,267
22	$27,267	$3,000	$3,632	$33,899
23	$33,899	$3,000	$4,428	$41,327
24	$41,327	$3,000	$5,319	$49,646
25	$49,646	$3,000	$6,318	$58,964
26	$58,964	$3,000	$7,436	$69,399
27	$69,399	$3,000	$8,688	$81,087
28	$81,087	$3,000	$10,090	$94,178
29	$94,178	$3,000	$11,661	$108,839
30	$108,839	$3,000	$13,421	$125,260
31	$125,260	$3,000	$15,391	$143,651
32	$143,651	$3,000	$17,598	$164,249
33	$164,249	$3,000	$20,070	$187,319
34	$187,319	$3,000	$22,838	$213,157
35	$213,157	$3,000	$25,939	$242,096
36	$242,096	$3,000	$29,412	$274,508
37	$274,508	$3,000	$33,301	$310,809
38	$310,809	$3,000	$37,657	$351,466
39	$351,466	$3,000	$42,536	$397,002
40	$397,002	$3,000	$48,000	$448,002
41	$448,002	$3,000	$54,120	$505,122
42	$505,122	$3,000	$60,975	$569,097
43	$569,097	$3,000	$68,652	$640,748
44	$640,748	$3,000	$77,250	$720,998
45	$720,998	$3,000	$86,880	$810,878
46	$810,878	$3,000	$97,665	$911,543
47	$911,543	$3,000	$109,745	$1,024,288
48	$1,024,288	$3,000	$123,275	$1,150,563
49	$1,150,563	$3,000	$138,428	$1,291,990
50	$1,291,990	$3,000	$155,399	$1,450,389
51	$1,450,389	$3,000	$174,407	$1,627,796
52	$1,627,796	$3,000	$195,696	$1,826,492
53	$1,826,492	$3,000	$219,539	$2,049,031
54	$2,049,031	$3,000	$246,244	$2,298,274
55	$2,298,274	$3,000	$276,153	$2,577,427
56	$2,577,427	$3,000	$309,651	$2,890,078
57	$2,890,078	$3,000	$347,169	$3,240,248
58	$3,240,248	$3,000	$389,190	$3,632,438
59	$3,632,438	$3,000	$436,253	$4,071,690
60	$4,071,690	$3,000	$488,963	$4,563,653
61	$4,563,653	$3,000	$547,998	$5,114,651
62	$5,114,651	$3,000	$614,118	$5,731,769

| Fig B: $3,000 Per Year With 10% Gains ||||
Age	Starting Balance	Contribution	Gain	End of Year
16	$0	$3,000	$300	$3,300
17	$3,300	$3,000	$630	$6,930
18	$6,930	$3,000	$993	$10,923
19	$10,923	$3,000	$1,392	$15,315
20	$15,315	$3,000	$1,832	$20,147
21	$20,147	$3,000	$2,315	$25,462
22	$25,462	$3,000	$2,846	$31,308
23	$31,308	$3,000	$3,431	$37,738
24	$37,738	$3,000	$4,074	$44,812
25	$44,812	$3,000	$4,781	$52,594
26	$52,594	$3,000	$5,559	$61,153
27	$61,153	$3,000	$6,415	$70,568
28	$70,568	$3,000	$7,357	$80,925
29	$80,925	$3,000	$8,392	$92,317
30	$92,317	$3,000	$9,532	$104,849
31	$104,849	$3,000	$10,785	$118,634
32	$118,634	$3,000	$12,163	$133,798
33	$133,798	$3,000	$13,680	$150,477
34	$150,477	$3,000	$15,348	$168,825
35	$168,825	$3,000	$17,182	$189,007
36	$189,007	$3,000	$19,201	$211,208
37	$211,208	$3,000	$21,421	$235,629
38	$235,629	$3,000	$23,863	$262,492
39	$262,492	$3,000	$26,549	$292,041
40	$292,041	$3,000	$29,504	$324,545
41	$324,545	$3,000	$32,755	$360,300
42	$360,300	$3,000	$36,330	$399,630
43	$399,630	$3,000	$40,263	$442,893
44	$442,893	$3,000	$44,589	$490,482
45	$490,482	$3,000	$49,348	$542,830
46	$542,830	$3,000	$54,583	$600,413
47	$600,413	$3,000	$60,341	$663,755
48	$663,755	$3,000	$66,675	$733,430
49	$733,430	$3,000	$73,643	$810,073
50	$810,073	$3,000	$81,307	$894,380
51	$894,380	$3,000	$89,738	$987,118
52	$987,118	$3,000	$99,012	$1,089,130
53	$1,089,130	$3,000	$109,213	$1,201,343
54	$1,201,343	$3,000	$120,434	$1,324,778
55	$1,324,778	$3,000	$132,778	$1,460,555
56	$1,460,555	$3,000	$146,356	$1,609,911
57	$1,609,911	$3,000	$161,291	$1,774,202
58	$1,774,202	$3,000	$177,720	$1,954,922
59	$1,954,922	$3,000	$195,792	$2,153,715
60	$2,153,715	$3,000	$215,671	$2,372,386
61	$2,372,386	$3,000	$237,539	$2,612,925
62	$2,612,925	$3,000	$261,592	$2,877,517

Fig C: $3,000 Per Year With 8% Gains

Age	Starting Balance	Contribution	Gain	End of Year
16	$0	$3,000	$240	$3,240
17	$3,240	$3,000	$499	$6,739
18	$6,739	$3,000	$779	$10,518
19	$10,518	$3,000	$1,081	$14,600
20	$14,600	$3,000	$1,408	$19,008
21	$19,008	$3,000	$1,761	$23,768
22	$23,768	$3,000	$2,141	$28,910
23	$28,910	$3,000	$2,553	$34,463
24	$34,463	$3,000	$2,997	$40,460
25	$40,460	$3,000	$3,477	$46,936
26	$46,936	$3,000	$3,995	$53,931
27	$53,931	$3,000	$4,555	$61,486
28	$61,486	$3,000	$5,159	$69,645
29	$69,645	$3,000	$5,812	$78,456
30	$78,456	$3,000	$6,517	$87,973
31	$87,973	$3,000	$7,278	$98,251
32	$98,251	$3,000	$8,100	$109,351
33	$109,351	$3,000	$8,988	$121,339
34	$121,339	$3,000	$9,947	$134,286
35	$134,286	$3,000	$10,983	$148,269
36	$148,269	$3,000	$12,102	$163,370
37	$163,370	$3,000	$13,310	$179,680
38	$179,680	$3,000	$14,614	$197,294
39	$197,294	$3,000	$16,024	$216,318
40	$216,318	$3,000	$17,545	$236,863
41	$236,863	$3,000	$19,189	$259,052
42	$259,052	$3,000	$20,964	$283,016
43	$283,016	$3,000	$22,881	$308,898
44	$308,898	$3,000	$24,952	$336,850
45	$336,850	$3,000	$27,188	$367,038
46	$367,038	$3,000	$29,603	$399,641
47	$399,641	$3,000	$32,211	$434,852
48	$434,852	$3,000	$35,028	$472,880
49	$472,880	$3,000	$38,070	$513,950
50	$513,950	$3,000	$41,356	$558,306
51	$558,306	$3,000	$44,905	$606,211
52	$606,211	$3,000	$48,737	$657,948
53	$657,948	$3,000	$52,876	$713,824
54	$713,824	$3,000	$57,346	$774,170
55	$774,170	$3,000	$62,174	$839,343
56	$839,343	$3,000	$67,387	$909,731
57	$909,731	$3,000	$73,018	$985,749
58	$985,749	$3,000	$79,100	$1,067,849
59	$1,067,849	$3,000	$85,668	$1,156,517
60	$1,156,517	$3,000	$92,761	$1,252,278
61	$1,252,278	$3,000	$100,422	$1,355,700
62	$1,355,700	$3,000	$108,696	$1,467,396

Fig D: $3,000 Per Year With 8% Gains

Age	Starting Balance	Contribution	Gain	End of Year
0	$0	$16,000	$1,280	$17,280
1	$17,280		$1,382	$18,662
2	$18,662		$1,493	$20,155
3	$20,155		$1,612	$21,768
4	$21,768		$1,741	$23,509
5	$23,509		$1,881	$25,390
6	$25,390		$2,031	$27,421
7	$27,421		$2,194	$29,615
8	$29,615		$2,369	$31,984
9	$31,984		$2,559	$34,543
10	$34,543		$2,763	$37,306
11	$37,306		$2,984	$40,291
12	$40,291		$3,223	$43,514
13	$43,514		$3,481	$46,995
14	$46,995		$3,760	$50,755
15	$50,755		$4,060	$54,815
16	$54,815		$4,385	$59,200
17	$59,200		$4,736	$63,936
18	$63,936		$5,115	$69,051
19	$69,051		$5,524	$74,575
20	$74,575		$5,966	$80,541
21	$80,541		$6,443	$86,985
22	$86,985		$6,959	$93,943
23	$93,943		$7,515	$101,459
24	$101,459		$8,117	$109,576
25	$109,576		$8,766	$118,342
26	$118,342		$9,467	$127,809
27	$127,809		$10,225	$138,034
28	$138,034		$11,043	$149,076
29	$149,076		$11,926	$161,003
30	$161,003		$12,880	$173,883
31	$173,883		$13,911	$187,793
32	$187,793		$15,023	$202,817
33	$202,817		$16,225	$219,042
34	$219,042		$17,523	$236,566
35	$236,566		$18,925	$255,491
36	$255,491		$20,439	$275,930
37	$275,930		$22,074	$298,004
38	$298,004		$23,840	$321,845
39	$321,845		$25,748	$347,592
40	$347,592		$27,807	$375,400
41	$375,400		$30,032	$405,432
42	$405,432		$32,435	$437,866
43	$437,866		$35,029	$472,896
44	$472,896		$37,832	$510,727
45	$510,727		$40,858	$551,585
46	$551,585		$44,127	$595,712

Fig D: $3,000 Per Year With 8% Gains			
Age	Starting Balance	Contribution	Gain	End of Year
47	$595,712		$47,657	$643,369
48	$643,369		$51,470	$694,839
49	$694,839		$55,587	$750,426
50	$750,426		$60,034	$810,460
51	$810,460		$64,837	$875,297
52	$875,297		$70,024	$945,320
53	$945,320		$75,626	$1,020,946
54	$1,020,946		$81,676	$1,102,622
55	$1,102,622		$88,210	$1,190,831
56	$1,190,831		$95,267	$1,286,098
57	$1,286,098		$102,888	$1,388,986
58	$1,388,986		$111,119	$1,500,105
59	$1,500,105		$120,008	$1,620,113
60	$1,620,113		$129,609	$1,749,722
61	$1,749,722		$139,978	$1,889,700
62	$1,889,700		$151,176	$2,040,876
63	$2,040,876		$163,270	$2,204,146
64	$2,204,146		$176,332	$2,380,478
65	$2,380,478		$190,438	$2,570,916

Fig E: $16,000 Per Year With 8% Gains Starting At 33				
Age	Starting Balance	Contribution	Gain	End of Year
33	$0	$16,000	$1,280	$17,280
34	$17,280	$16,000	$2,662	$35,942
35	$35,942	$16,000	$4,155	$56,098
36	$56,098	$16,000	$5,768	$77,866
37	$77,866	$16,000	$7,509	$101,375
38	$101,375	$16,000	$9,390	$126,765
39	$126,765	$16,000	$11,421	$154,186
40	$154,186	$16,000	$13,615	$183,801
41	$183,801	$16,000	$15,984	$215,785
42	$215,785	$16,000	$18,543	$250,328
43	$250,328	$16,000	$21,306	$287,634
44	$287,634	$16,000	$24,291	$327,925
45	$327,925	$16,000	$27,514	$371,439
46	$371,439	$16,000	$30,995	$418,434
47	$418,434	$16,000	$34,755	$469,189
48	$469,189	$16,000	$38,815	$524,004
49	$524,004	$16,000	$43,200	$583,204
50	$583,204	$16,000	$47,936	$647,140
51	$647,140	$16,000	$53,051	$716,191
52	$716,191	$16,000	$58,575	$790,767
53	$790,767	$16,000	$64,541	$871,308
54	$871,308	$16,000	$70,985	$958,293
55	$958,293	$16,000	$77,943	$1,052,236
56	$1,052,236	$16,000	$85,459	$1,153,695
57	$1,153,695	$16,000	$93,576	$1,263,271
58	$1,263,271	$16,000	$102,342	$1,381,612
59	$1,381,612	$16,000	$111,809	$1,509,421
60	$1,509,421	$16,000	$122,034	$1,647,455
61	$1,647,455	$16,000	$133,076	$1,796,531
62	$1,796,531	$16,000	$145,003	$1,957,534
63	$1,957,534	$16,000	$157,883	$2,131,417
64	$2,131,417	$16,000	$171,793	$2,319,210
65	$2,319,210	$16,000	$186,817	$2,522,027

Fig F: $3,000 Per Year With 8% Gains Starting At 35			
Age	Starting Balance	Contribution	Gain	End of Year
35	$0	$3,000	$240	$3,240
36	$3,240	$3,000	$499	$6,739
37	$6,739	$3,000	$779	$10,518
38	$10,518	$3,000	$1,081	$14,600
39	$14,600	$3,000	$1,408	$19,008
40	$19,008	$3,000	$1,761	$23,768
41	$23,768	$3,000	$2,141	$28,910
42	$28,910	$3,000	$2,553	$34,463
43	$34,463	$3,000	$2,997	$40,460
44	$40,460	$3,000	$3,477	$46,936
45	$46,936	$3,000	$3,995	$53,931
46	$53,931	$3,000	$4,555	$61,486
47	$61,486	$3,000	$5,159	$69,645
48	$69,645	$3,000	$5,812	$78,456
49	$78,456	$3,000	$6,517	$87,973
50	$87,973	$3,000	$7,278	$98,251
51	$98,251	$3,000	$8,100	$109,351
52	$109,351	$3,000	$8,988	$121,339
53	$121,339	$3,000	$9,947	$134,286
54	$134,286	$3,000	$10,983	$148,269
55	$148,269	$3,000	$12,102	$163,370
56	$163,370	$3,000	$13,310	$179,680
57	$179,680	$3,000	$14,614	$197,294
58	$197,294	$3,000	$16,024	$216,318
59	$216,318	$3,000	$17,545	$236,863
60	$236,863	$3,000	$19,189	$259,052
61	$259,052	$3,000	$20,964	$283,016
62	$283,016	$3,000	$22,881	$308,898
63	$308,898	$3,000	$24,952	$336,850
64	$336,850	$3,000	$27,188	$367,038
65	$367,038	$3,000	$29,603	$399,641

Fig G: Staying At Home And Saving $10K Per Year After HS					
Age	Starting Balance	Contribution	Parent Match	Gain	End of Year
16	$0	$2,000	$1,000	$240	$3,240
17	$3,240	$3,000	$1,500	$619	$8,359
18	$8,359	$10,000	$5,000	$1,869	$25,228
19	$25,228	$10,000	$5,000	$3,218	$43,446
20	$43,446	$10,000	$5,000	$4,676	$63,122
21	$63,122	$10,000	$5,000	$6,250	$84,372
22	$84,372			$6,750	$91,121
23	$91,121			$7,290	$98,411
24	$98,411			$7,873	$106,284
25	$106,284			$8,503	$114,787
26	$114,787			$9,183	$123,970
27	$123,970			$9,918	$133,887
28	$133,887			$10,711	$144,598
29	$144,598			$11,568	$156,166
30	$156,166			$12,493	$168,659
31	$168,659			$13,493	$182,152
32	$182,152			$14,572	$196,724
33	$196,724			$15,738	$212,462
34	$212,462			$16,997	$229,459
35	$229,459			$18,357	$247,816
36	$247,816			$19,825	$267,641
37	$267,641			$21,411	$289,052
38	$289,052			$23,124	$312,176
39	$312,176			$24,974	$337,151
40	$337,151			$26,972	$364,123
41	$364,123			$29,130	$393,252
42	$393,252			$31,460	$424,713
43	$424,713			$33,977	$458,690
44	$458,690			$36,695	$495,385
45	$495,385			$39,631	$535,016
46	$535,016			$42,801	$577,817
47	$577,817			$46,225	$624,042
48	$624,042			$49,923	$673,966
49	$673,966			$53,917	$727,883
50	$727,883			$58,231	$786,114
51	$786,114			$62,889	$849,003
52	$849,003			$67,920	$916,923
53	$916,923			$73,354	$990,277
54	$990,277			$79,222	$1,069,499
55	$1,069,499			$85,560	$1,155,059
56	$1,155,059			$92,405	$1,247,463
57	$1,247,463			$99,797	$1,347,260
58	$1,347,260			$107,781	$1,455,041
59	$1,455,041			$116,403	$1,571,445
60	$1,571,445			$125,716	$1,697,160
61	$1,697,160			$135,773	$1,832,933
62	$1,832,933			$146,635	$1,979,568

FOR MY CHILDREN'S CHILDREN

Fig H:Staying At Home And Saving $10K Per Year After HS And Continuing					
Age	Starting Balance	Contribution	Parent Match	Gain	End of Year
16	$0	$2,000	$1,000	$240	$3,240
17	$3,240	$3,000	$1,500	$619	$8,359
18	$8,359	$10,000	$5,000	$1,869	$25,228
19	$25,228	$10,000	$5,000	$3,218	$43,446
20	$43,446	$10,000	$5,000	$4,676	$63,122
21	$63,122	$10,000	$5,000	$6,250	$84,372
22	$84,372	$10,000		$7,550	$101,921
23	$101,921	$10,000		$8,954	$120,875
24	$120,875	$10,000		$10,470	$141,345
25	$141,345	$10,000		$12,108	$163,453
26	$163,453	$10,000		$13,876	$187,329
27	$187,329	$10,000		$15,786	$213,115
28	$213,115	$10,000		$17,849	$240,964
29	$240,964	$10,000		$20,077	$271,042
30	$271,042	$10,000		$22,483	$303,525
31	$303,525	$10,000		$25,082	$338,607
32	$338,607	$10,000		$27,889	$376,495
33	$376,495	$10,000		$30,920	$417,415
34	$417,415	$10,000		$34,193	$461,608
35	$461,608	$10,000		$37,729	$509,337
36	$509,337	$10,000		$41,547	$560,884
37	$560,884	$10,000		$45,671	$616,555
38	$616,555	$10,000		$50,124	$676,679
39	$676,679	$10,000		$54,934	$741,613
40	$741,613	$10,000		$60,129	$811,742
41	$811,742	$10,000		$65,739	$887,482
42	$887,482	$10,000		$71,799	$969,280
43	$969,280	$10,000		$78,342	$1,057,623
44	$1,057,623	$10,000		$85,410	$1,153,032
45	$1,153,032	$10,000		$93,043	$1,256,075
46	$1,256,075	$10,000		$101,286	$1,367,361
47	$1,367,361	$10,000		$110,189	$1,487,550
48	$1,487,550	$10,000		$119,804	$1,617,354
49	$1,617,354	$10,000		$130,188	$1,757,542
50	$1,757,542	$10,000		$141,403	$1,908,946
51	$1,908,946	$10,000		$153,516	$2,072,461
52	$2,072,461	$10,000		$166,597	$2,249,058
53	$2,249,058	$10,000		$180,725	$2,439,783
54	$2,439,783	$10,000		$195,983	$2,645,765
55	$2,645,765	$10,000		$212,461	$2,868,227
56	$2,868,227	$10,000		$230,258	$3,108,485
57	$3,108,485	$10,000		$249,479	$3,367,964
58	$3,367,964	$10,000		$270,237	$3,648,201
59	$3,648,201	$10,000		$292,656	$3,950,857
60	$3,950,857	$10,000		$316,869	$4,277,725
61	$4,277,725	$10,000		$343,018	$4,630,743
62	$4,630,743	$10,000		$371,259	$5,012,003

Age	Starting Balance	Contribution	Parent Match	Gain	End of Year
\multicolumn{6}{c}{Fig I: $100 Per month 0-18 plus saving ½ income from 6 to 18}
0	$0	$0	$1,200	$96	$1,296
1	$1,296	$0	$1,200	$200	$2,696
2	$2,696	$0	$1,200	$312	$4,207
3	$4,207	$0	$1,200	$433	$5,840
4	$5,840	$0	$1,200	$563	$7,603
5	$7,603	$0	$1,200	$704	$9,507
6	$9,507	$250	$1,200	$877	$11,834
7	$11,834	$250	$1,200	$1,063	$14,347
8	$14,347	$250	$1,200	$1,264	$17,060
9	$17,060	$500	$1,200	$1,501	$20,261
10	$20,261	$500	$1,200	$1,757	$23,718
11	$23,718	$500	$1,200	$2,033	$27,452
12	$27,452	$1,000	$1,200	$2,372	$32,024
13	$32,024	$1,000	$1,200	$2,738	$36,962
14	$36,962	$2,000	$1,200	$3,213	$43,375
15	$43,375	$2,000	$1,200	$3,726	$50,301
16	$50,301	$3,000	$1,200	$4,360	$58,861
17	$58,861	$5,000	$1,200	$5,205	$70,265
18	$70,265	$5,000	$1,200	$6,117	$82,583
19	$82,583			$6,607	$89,189
20	$89,189			$7,135	$96,324
21	$96,324			$7,706	$104,030
22	$104,030			$8,322	$112,353
23	$112,353			$8,988	$121,341
24	$121,341			$9,707	$131,048
25	$131,048			$10,484	$141,532
26	$141,532			$11,323	$152,855
27	$152,855			$12,228	$165,083
28	$165,083			$13,207	$178,290
29	$178,290			$14,263	$192,553
30	$192,553			$15,404	$207,957
31	$207,957			$16,637	$224,594
32	$224,594			$17,967	$242,561
33	$242,561			$19,405	$261,966
34	$261,966			$20,957	$282,923
35	$282,923			$22,634	$305,557
36	$305,557			$24,445	$330,002
37	$330,002			$26,400	$356,402
38	$356,402			$28,512	$384,914
39	$384,914			$30,793	$415,707
40	$415,707			$33,257	$448,964
41	$448,964			$35,917	$484,881
42	$484,881			$38,790	$523,671
43	$523,671			$41,894	$565,565
44	$565,565			$45,245	$610,810
45	$610,810			$48,865	$659,675
46	$659,675			$52,774	$712,449

FOR MY CHILDREN'S CHILDREN

Age	Fig I: $100 Per month 0-18 plus saving ½ income from 6 to 18				
	Starting Balance	Contribution	Parent Match	Gain	End of Year
47	$712,449			$56,996	$769,445
48	$769,445			$61,556	$831,001
49	$831,001			$66,480	$897,481
50	$897,481			$71,798	$969,279
51	$969,279			$77,542	$1,046,821
52	$1,046,821			$83,746	$1,130,567
53	$1,130,567			$90,445	$1,221,012
54	$1,221,012			$97,681	$1,318,693
55	$1,318,693			$105,495	$1,424,189
56	$1,424,189			$113,935	$1,538,124
57	$1,538,124			$123,050	$1,661,174
58	$1,661,174			$132,894	$1,794,068
59	$1,794,068			$143,525	$1,937,593
60	$1,937,593			$155,007	$2,092,601
61	$2,092,601			$167,408	$2,260,009
62	$2,260,009			$180,801	$2,440,809
63	$2,440,809			$195,265	$2,636,074
64	$2,636,074			$210,886	$2,846,960
65	$2,846,960			$227,757	$3,074,717

www.ingramcontent.com/pod-product-compliance
Lightning Source LLC
Chambersburg PA
CBHW060838220526
45466CB00003B/1155